HOW
SOCCER
EXPLAINS
THE WORLD

HOW SOCCER EXPLAINS THE WORLD

An Unlikely Theory of Globalization

Franklin Foer

HarperCollins*Publishers*

HarperCollins books may be purchased for educational, business, or sales promotional use. For information, please write: Special Markets Department, HarperCollins Publishers Inc., 10 East 53rd Street, New York, NY 10022.

FIRST EDITION

Designed by Laura Lindgren

Printed on acid-free paper

Library of Congress Cataloging-in-Publication Data is available upon request.

ISBN 0-06-621234-0

04 05 06 07 08 ❖/RRD 10 9 8 7 6 5

To Abby,
My Wife

And the Waimbergs,
My Brazilian Cousins

Contents

HOW
SOCCER
EXPLAINS
THE WORLD

Prologue

I suck at soccer.

When I was a boy, my parents would turn their backs to the field to avoid watching me play. I don't blame them. The game's fundamental principles only dawned on me slowly, after I had spent many seasons running in the opposite direction of the ball.

Despite these traumas, or perhaps because of them, my love for soccer later developed into something quite mad. I desperately wanted to master the game that had been the source of so much childhood shame. Because I would never achieve competence in the game itself, I could do the next best thing, to try and acquire a maven's understanding. For an American, this wasn't easy. During my childhood, public television would irregularly rebroadcast matches from Germany and Italy at televangelist hours on Sunday mornings. Those measly offerings would have to carry you through the four years between World Cups. That was it.

But slowly, technology filled in the gaps. First, praise God, came the Internet, where you could read the British sports pages and closely follow the players that you had encountered at the World Cup. Then Rupert Murdoch, blessed be his name, created a cable channel called Fox Sports World, dedicated almost entirely to airing European and Latin American soccer.* Now, a rooftop dish brings into my living room a feed from the Spanish club Real Madrid's cable channel, as well as games from Paraguay, Honduras, the Netherlands, Scotland, and France, not to mention Brazil, Argentina, and England.

At about the same time these television stations began consuming disturbingly large chunks of my leisure time, op-ed columnists and economists began to talk about the era of globalization. Because I spend many of my non-soccer-watching hours as a political journalist in Washington, I found myself drawn into the thick of this discussion. Thanks to the collapse of trade barriers and new technologies, the world was said to have become much more interdependent. Thomas Friedman, the *New York Times* columnist and high priest of this new order, hailed "the inexorable integration of markets, nation-states and technologies to a degree never witnessed before—in a way that is enabling individuals, corporations and nation-states to reach around the world farther, faster, deeper and cheaper than ever before."

As a soccer fan, I understood exactly what he meant. It wasn't just the ways in which the Internet and satellites had made the world of soccer so much smaller and more accessible. You could see globalization on the pitch: During the nineties, Basque teams, under the stewardship of Welsh coaches, stocked up on Dutch and Turkish players; Moldavian squads imported

---

*Yes, this book owes its existence to the beneficence of Rupert Murdoch and his company, HarperCollins.

Nigerians. Everywhere you looked, it suddenly seemed, national borders and national identities had been swept into the dustbin of soccer history. The best clubs* now competed against one another on a near-weekly basis in transnational tournaments like the European Champions League or Latin America's Copa Libertadores.

It was easy to be wildly enthusiastic about the new order. These tournaments were a fan's sweet dream: the chance to see Juventus of Turin play Bayern Munich one week and Barcelona the next. When coaches created cultural alchemies out of their rosters, they often yielded wonderful new spectacles: The cynical, defensive-minded Italian style livened by an infusion of freewheeling Dutchmen and Brazilians; the English stiff-upper-lip style (or lack of style) tempered by a bit of continental flair, brought across the Channel in the form of French strikers. From the perspective of my couch, the game seemed much further along in the process of globalization than any other economy on the planet.

What's more, I could think of a further benefit of soccer's globalization that had yet to be realized: Someone needed to write a book on the subject that would require the (oh-so-arduous) task of traveling the world, attending soccer matches, watching training sessions, and interviewing his heroes. For eight months, I took a leave from my job at the *New Republic* magazine and visited the stadiums that I most desperately wanted to see.

---

*Clubs, like Manchester United and Real Madrid, are different from the national teams that assemble to compete in quadrennial World Cups and other international tournaments, although the best players play on both.

At about the time that I started working on this
book, in the fall of 2001, the consensus on globalization changed considerably—for obvious reasons. It was
no longer possible to speak so breathlessly, so messian-
ically of the political promise of economic interdependence. And there was another problem. The world's
brief experiment in interdependence didn't come close
to delivering the advertised result of prosperity. This
book tries to use the metaphor of soccer to address
some of the nagging questions about this failure: Why
have some nations remained poor, even though they
had so much foreign investment coursing through
them? How dangerous are the multinational corporations that the Left rails against?

This is not to dredge up the tired old Marxist criticisms of corporate capitalism—the big question of the
book is less economic than cultural. The innovation of
the anti-globalization left is its embrace of traditional-
ism: its worry that global tastes and brands will steam-
roll indigenous cultures. Of course, soccer isn't the
same as Bach or Buddhism. But it is often more deeply
felt than religion, and just as much a part of the community's fabric, a repository of traditions. During
Franco's rule, the clubs Athletic Bilbao and Real
Sociedad were the only venues where Basque people
could express their cultural pride without winding up
in jail. In English industrial towns like Coventry and
Derby, soccer clubs helped glue together small cities
amid oppressive dinginess.

By the logic of both its critics and proponents, the
global culture should have wiped away these local
institutions. Indeed, traveling the world, it's hard not to

be awed by the power of mega-brands like the clubs Manchester United and Real Madrid, backed by Nike and Adidas, who have cultivated support across continents, prying fans away from their old allegiances. But that homogenization turned out to be more of an exception than I had anticipated. Wandering among lunatic fans, gangster owners, and crazed Bulgarian strikers, I kept noticing the ways that globalization had failed to diminish the game's local cultures, local blood feuds, and even local corruption. In fact, I began to suspect that globalization had actually increased the power of these local entities—and not always in such a good way.

On my travels, I tried to use soccer—its fans, its players, and strategies—as a way of thinking about how people would identify themselves in this new era. Would they embrace new, more globalized labels? Would people stop thinking of themselves as English and Brazilian and begin to define themselves as Europeans and Latin Americans? Or would those new identities be meaningless, with shallow roots in history? Would people revert back to older identities, like religion and tribe? If soccer is an object lesson, then perhaps religion and tribe have too much going for them.

This book has three parts. The first tries to explain the failure of globalization to erode ancient hatreds in the game's great rivalries. It is the hooligan-heavy section of the book. The second part uses soccer to address economics: the consequences of migration, the persistence of corruption, and the rise of powerful new oligarchs like Silvio Berlusconi, the president of Italy and the AC Milan club. Finally, the book uses soccer to defend the virtues of old-fashioned nationalism—a way to blunt the return of tribalism.

The story begins bleakly and grows progressively more optimistic. In the end, I found it hard to be too hostile toward globalization. For all its many faults, it has brought soccer to the far corners of the world and into my life.

1

How Soccer Explains the Gangster's Paradise

I.

Red Star Belgrade is the most beloved, most successful soccer team in Serbia. Like nearly every club in Europe and Latin America, it has a following of unruly fans capable of terrific violence. But at Red Star the violent fans occupy a place of honor, and more than that. They meet with club officials to streamline the organizational flow chart of their gangs. Their leaders receive stipends. And as part of this package, they have access to office space in the team's headquarters in the upper-middle-class neighborhood of Topcider.

The gangs have influence, in large measure, because they've won it with intimidation. A few months before I arrived in Belgrade to learn about the club's complicity in the Balkan Wars of the 1990s, Red Star fan clubs had burst into the team's training session. With bats, bars, and other bludgeons, they beat three of their own players. After their havoc, they aren't typically shy about advertising their accomplishments. In this instance, the hooligans told reporters bluntly that they could "no longer tolerate lack of commitment on the pitch." It took only one phone call to organize an interview with a handful of them in their first-floor meeting room at the Red Star headquarters.

The Belgrade neighborhood around Red Star is cartoonishly ominous. An enormous gaggle of crows resides on the stadium's roof. When goals are scored and the crowd erupts, the birds flee—across town, it's possible to gauge the results of a game based on presence or absence of an ornithological cloud above the skyline. On the other side of the street from the stadium, the family of Arkan, the most notorious warlord and gangster in Serb history, lives in a castle he constructed, a nouveau riche monstrosity with tiers of towers and turrets. When I loiter near the house for too long, a large man in a leather jacket emerges and inquires about my business. Because of the atrocities committed by Arkan's men, I describe myself as a lost tourist, nervously ask him for directions, and walk away briskly. On the evening of my visit, the sky is gunmetal.

My translator had arranged for me to meet with Draza, a leader of a Red Star fan club that calls itself the Ultra Bad Boys. He had persuaded him with the overblown promise that an interview would bring glory unto the club and world renown unto the achievements of the Red Star fans. Six of Draza's loquacious colleagues join him. At first glance, the Bad Boys look entirely unworthy of the first part of their name and too worthy of the second. Aside from the big red tattoos of their gang name on their calves, they seem like relatively upstanding young men. Draza wears a fleece jacket and chinos. His head of overgrown yet obviously manicured hair has the aura of a freshman philosophy student. As it turns out, he *is* a college student, swamped with preparations for exams. His comrades aren't any more menacing. One of them has a bowl haircut, a pudgy face, and an oversized ski parka that he never removes—he looks like the kind of guy who's been shoved into his fair share of lockers.

Perhaps to increase their credibility, the Bad Boys have brought along a gray-haired man called Krle, who wears a ratty black San Antonio Spurs jacket. Krle's sinewy frame gives the impression that he fills his leisure time with pull-ups on a door frame in his flat. Many years of living a hooligan life have aged him prematurely. (When I ask his age and occupation, he changes the subject.) Unlike the naïve enthusiasm exhibited by the teens, who greet me warmly, Krle blares indifference. He tells my translator that he has only joined our interview because Draza insisted. His one gesture of bonhomie is to continually pour me warm Serbian beer from a plastic bottle. After I taste the beer, it hardly seems like such a friendly gesture. But because of his angry gray eyes, I find myself drinking glass after glass.

Krle serves as senior advisor to the group, a mentor to the aspiring hooligans. Putting aside his intense glare and unfriendly demeanor, I was actually glad for his presence. My interest in Red Star centers on the 1990s, his heyday as thug, when the fan clubs played a pivotal role in the revival of Serbian nationalism—the idea that the Serbs are eternal victims of history who must fight to preserve a shred of their dignity. With little prodding, Draza speaks openly about the connections. Unfortunately, his monologue doesn't last long. Exerting his authority with volatile glances and brusque interruptions, Krle seizes control of the conversation. He answers questions curtly.

"Who do you hate most?"

A pause for a few seconds' worth of consideration. "A Croatian, a cop: it doesn't make a difference. I'd kill them all."

"What's your preferred method for beating a guy?"

"Metal bars, a special kick that breaks a leg, when a guy's not noticing." He sharply stomps down a leg, an obviously well-practiced move.

Because the beer has kicked in, I try to get closer to the reason for my visit. "I noticed that you call Arkan 'commandant.' Could you tell me a little more about how he organized the fans?"

His look is one of deep offense and then unmitigated fury. Even before the translation comes, his meaning is clear. "I shouldn't be answering your questions. You're an American. And your country bombed us. You killed good Serb men."

As good a reason as any to redirect the conversation to another topic. In an aside to my translator, which he didn't tell me about until after our interview, Krle announces, "If I met this American asshole on the street, I'd beat the shit out of him." Krle then drops out of the conversation. At first, he stands impatiently on the far side of the room. Then he plops into a chair and leans back on its hind legs. When this ceases to hold his attention, he stands again and paces.

In the meantime, his protégés continue their enthusiastic descriptions of violence. They tell me their
favorite guerilla tactic: dressing in the opposition's jersey. This enables them to befriend visiting fans, lure
them into their cars, transport them to remote locales,
and beat them. They boast about their domination of
fans from Partizan, their Belgrade rivals. Draza especially relishes describing a game against Partizan the
previous season. Thirty minutes before kick off, the
Ultra Bad Boys had quietly gathered their toughest guys
at one end of the stadium by a small outcropping of
trees. Each thug carried a metal bar or wooden bat.
They formed a V-shaped formation and began to ram-
page their way around the stadium, beating anyone in
their path. First, they attacked the visiting fans. Then,
they slugged their way through a horde of police. The
Ultra Bad Boys attacked so quickly that neither the cops
nor the Partizan fans had time to respond. In their
path, they left lines of casualties, like the fresh tracks of
a lawnmower. "We made it around the stadium in five
minutes," says Draza. "It was incredible."

Aside from Krle's paroxysms, the Ultra Bad Boys
never curse. They consider themselves to occupy higher
moral terrain than their foes: no use of firearms, no
beating of the enemy after he loses consciousness.
Draza explains, "Partizan fans once killed a fifteen-year-
old Red Star supporter. He was sitting in the stadium,
and they fired flares at his chest. Those monsters killed
the boy. They observe no limits." The Ultra Bad Boys
speak until they exhaust my questions.

As I put away my pen and notebook, Krle reengages
the group. He stands over me and demonstrates the

three-fingered salute of Serb nationalism, the peace sign plus a thumb. The gesture signifies both the holy trinity and the Serb belief that they are the planet's most authentic representatives of the holy trinity. "Now you," he says in English. I comply. Before I leave the room, Krle makes me repeat the gesture four more times. When I later describe this moment to a human rights activist who has spent many years in Belgrade, he tells me that, during the war, paramilitaries forced Muslims and Croats to make this salute before their rape or murder.

Krle had been a Red Star thug during the club's most glorious year. In 1991, the team won the European Champions Cup—the most prestigious annual prize in club competition. That team had been a metaphor for the crumbling hulk of Yugoslavia. Despite its history as a vehicle for Serb nationalism, Red Star had included players from across the country, even a vociferous Croatian separatist. Each state of the old Yugoslavia had developed widely accepted ethnic stereotypes that sports commentators then transposed to its players. Slovenians were superb defenders, tirelessly trailing opposing forwards. Croatians possessed a Germanic penchant for pouncing on scoring opportunities. Bosnians and Serbs were creative dribblers and passers, but occasionally lacking in tactical acumen. At Red Star, an amalgam of disparate Yugoslavs bundled their specialties and beat the superpowers of Western Europe.

This performance should have given a modicum of hope for the salvage of multi-ethnic Yugoslavia. But in the shadow of this championship season, in Red Star's headquarters and stadium, the destruction of this

Yugoslavia was being plotted. From Red Star's own ranks, a hooligan paramilitary force was organized and armed. Krle, who took a bullet in his leg, would serve in this army. The Red Star fans would become Milosevic's shock troops, the most active agents of ethnic cleansing, highly efficient practitioners of genocide.

It's hard to imagine that Ultra Bad Boys are typical figures. They seem a product of a war-torn country and its diseased ideology. But they're really not such a homegrown oddity. Starting in the 1980s, the soccer hooligan widely came to be considered a leading enemy of the West. "A disgrace to civilized society," Margaret Thatcher once said. Based on death toll—more than one hundred in the 1980s—the English were the world's leading producer of deranged fans, but they were far from alone. Throughout Europe, Latin America, and Africa, violence had become part of soccer's culture. And even in places where violence had long accompanied soccer, it became more widespread and destructive in the eighties and nineties. The Serbian fans were merely a bit better organized and much better armed than the rest of the world.

Susan Faludi and a phalanx of sociologists have an explanation for this outburst. They have written about downsized men, the ones whose industrial jobs were outsourced to third-world labor. Deprived of traditional work and knocked off patriarchal pedestals, these men desperately wanted to reassert their masculinity. Soccer violence gave them a rare opportunity to actually exert control. When these fans dabbled in racism and radical nationalism, it was because those ideologies worked as metaphors for their own lives. Their nations and races had been victimized by the world just as badly as they had been themselves.

Economic deprivation and displacement are obvious explanations. But there's so much these factors can't explain. Ultra Bad Boys like Draza can also be college boys with decent prospects. The Chelsea Headhunters, the most notorious English hooligan gang, include stockbrokers and middle-class thrill seekers. Besides, human history is filled with poor people, and rarely do they get together in groups to maim for maiming's sake.

Something different happened in this era. An ethos of gangsterism—spread by movies, music, and fashion—conquered the world. The Red Star fans modeled themselves after foreigners they admired, especially the Western European hooligans. The name Ultra Bad Boys was ripped off from Italian supporters' clubs. Another fan club called itself the Red Devils, after British club Manchester United's nickname. In the late eighties and early nineties, the Red Star hooligans would go to the British Cultural Center in downtown Belgrade to scan the papers for the latest antics of English hooligans. The Serb hooligans also paid tribute with their fashion. They wore Adidas track suits, gold chains, and white leather sneakers, just like the crazed fans they read about on the other side of the continent. Of course, the genealogy of this aesthetic had other roots than England. It borrowed heavily from African American gangster rap, a favorite genre of Serb youth, and filched mores from the emerging Russian mafia. Gangsterism and its nihilistic violence had become fully globalized. And it was in the Balkans that this sub-culture became the culture and unfolded toward its logical conclusion.

II.

In the history of hooligan warfare, no battle has been quite so spectacular. A year before Red Star lifted its European Cup, it traveled to Croatia for a match against the rival club Dinamo Zagreb. Signs that the multi-ethnic state of Yugoslavia might not have much more life could be seen all around Zagreb. Two weeks earlier, the Croats had elected the ultranationalist Franjo Tudjman, a former general and former president of the Partizan Belgrade soccer club. Tudjman's adoption of Ustache icons—the symbols of the Croatian fascists who collaborated with Nazis to kill hundreds of thousands of Serbs—roused the long-dormant national passions of his people.

During the thirty-five years the charismatic communist Marshal Tito ruled Yugoslavia, he had suppressed bad feelings over World War II, simply declaring the expression of such feelings illegal. Yugoslavia had never come to terms with the fact that its two largest constituents had slaughtered one another. Now, with communism dissolving, the old wounds reopened. Serbs and Croats began to openly expose one another's war crimes—and demand justice for them. A rush of breathless revisionist literature described the "hidden history" of World War II. The books were turned into TV documentaries. And the TV documentaries were reduced to potent political slogans that moved the national agendas in nationalist directions. As one of his first acts, Tudjman "demoted" Serbs from the Croatian constitution. The new, or rather old, enmity could be seen visibly at the soccer stadium. In matches between Serb and Croat teams, fans sang about their respective slaughters.

The match between Red Star and Dinamo, however, was the first time in fifty years that Yugoslavia had seen its ethnic groups openly battle one another. At first, the trouble seemed manageable by the standards of the European game. Red Star fans ripped down billboards and shouted, "We will kill Tudjman." When the Dinamo fans began throwing stones at them, the Red Star fans used the billboards as shields. Fences that separated the opposing fans mysteriously disappeared. A brawl engulfed the entire stadium, with the combatants identified by the color of their shirts, and then moved onto the field. The police handled the situation with ineptitude. As a cop beat a Zagreb fan, a Dinamo player called Zvonimir Boban intervened with a flying kick into the officer's gut. Helicopters descended on the stadium to evacuate the Serb players from the melee.

To anyone watching, it was clear that both Serbs and Croats had come ready to fight. Rocks had been carefully stockpiled in the stadium before the game, waiting to be thrown. Acid had been strategically stored so that Croatian fans could burn through the fences separating them from their Serbian counterparts. Standing next to the Red Star coach, guarding him from the violence, was an even more ominous presence, a secret-police hit man called Zeljko Raznatovic. Through his career as a gangster, he'd reached mythical proportions, so much so that everyone simply referred to him by one of his approximately forty aliases. Considering all the Muslims he would later massacre, it is ironic that he went by the Turkish name Arkan.

Arkan came of age in the placidity of Tito's Yugoslavia, a Balkan's version of June-and-Ward's America, where Serbs and Croats were supposed to be happy neighbors. But Arkan had bucked communist conformism. His father had served as an officer in Tito's air force and used the military rulebook as a Dr. Spock–like guide for raising his son. Predictably, the harsh discipline backfired. By about age sixteen, Arkan had dropped out of a naval academy, stowed away to Italy, and taken up life as a petty criminal in Paris. Not long into this stint, he was nabbed and sentenced to three years in juvenile detention. Unlike the other Yugoslav criminals with whom he teamed, Arkan hadn't become a thief to fund a luxurious gangster lifestyle. One of his cronies recounted celebrating a heist in Milan with whiskey and whores. Arkan refused to join the party. He sat alone in a room with the window open, letting cigarette smoke escape, performing calisthenics.

The myth of Arkan has more to do with the aftermath of crimes than the crimes themselves. He had a magical capacity for escape. In 1974, the Belgians locked him up for armed robbery. Three years later, he broke free from prison and fled to Holland. When the Dutch police caught him, he somehow managed to slither away from prison again. That same year, he repeated the feat at a German prison hospital. The masterpiece in this oeuvre was his appearance at the Swedish trial of his partner Carlo Fabiani. Arkan burst into the courtroom carrying a gun in each hand. He aimed one at the judge and tossed the other to Fabianni. Their audacious escape through a courtroom window could have been orchestrated by Jerry Bruckheimer.

With such attention-grabbing escapades, Western Europe became too hot for Arkan. Back in Belgrade, he reconciled with his father and then worked his connections to the Yugoslav security apparatus. Well before Arkan's return, the police had begun recruiting criminals to perform dirty work, mostly assassinating exiled dissidents. As part of the government arrangement, the criminals could violate the law abroad and then return to haven in Yugoslavia. Arkan became a star in this system, and he flaunted his status. He drove through Belgrade in a pink Cadillac. After he killed a cop, an extremely rare occurrence in the well-ordered communist society, he unsheathed his Ministry of Interior credentials and casually walked out of his trial.

In his brash manner, Arkan had prefigured the late-eighties transition away from communism, an epoch when gangsters and smugglers came to rule the booming Serb economy. And he was more than just a representative figure. He helped Slobodan Milosevic, who became the Serbian Communist Party boss in 1986, manage an exceptionally tricky task. Milosevic had amassed popularity and power by exploiting the long-suppressed nationalism of the Serbs. But as a cynic he also understood how quickly these inflamed passions could turn against him. Nationalism needed to be carefully regulated. One glaring danger spot was the Red Star Belgrade stadium, where the team's hooligans had become politicized. They had begun lofting placards with the faces of Serbian Orthodox saints and the ultra-nationalist novelist Vuk Draskovic, head of the Serbian Renewal Party. Their chants called for secession: "Serbia, not Yugoslavia."

It wasn't strange that the stadium should become so fervent. From the start, Red Star had been a bastion of nationalism. Under communism, eastern-bloc soccer clubs adhered to basically the same model of sponsorship. There was usually a team founded and supported by the army; another with the police as patrons; others aligned with trade unions and government ministries. In Belgrade, the army supported Partizan and the police backed Red Star. To Serb nationalists, the army represented the enemies of their cause. The ideology of the communist army rejected any notion of separate Serb identity as anathema to worker solidarity and ethnic harmony. Tito's partisans, the namesake of the army club, had murdered, jailed, and beat the Chetniks, the army of Serb nationalists (some say fascists) who had also battled the Nazis. It had suppressed the Serbian Orthodox church. With such odious opponents, Red Star became a home for those Serbs with aspirations of reclaiming their nation.

Throughout Red Star's history, police eminences sat on its board. In 1989, Milosevic's interior minister was there. The minister understood that Red Star had become a caldron of post-communist alienation and an uncontrollable mess of gangs, especially ultranationalist ones. Newspapers filled with stories decrying the stadiums as symbols of "general civilizational disintegration." To control the mess, the police tasked Arkan, a Red Star fanatic himself, with corralling the fans.

Arkan negotiated a truce among the warring factions, placing them all under one organization, with himself at the helm. Where Red Star fans had called themselves the "Gypsies"—an opponent's insult that they had turned into a badge of honor—Arkan renamed them Delije. Like Arkan's name, the new title derived from Turkish. It meant something close to heroes, and its distinctly martial connotations fit the new spirit of the club. Almost instantly, Arkan imposed the same discipline that he practiced in his own life. Petty acts of violence ceased. "Red Star's management proclaimed him its savior," one of the team's official magazines reported. Krle, who had become a foot soldier in the Delije, told me, "It was impossible not to have respect for a man like that."

As Arkan tamed the nationalists within Red Star, the political tides turned. Milosevic's nationalist rhetoric had convinced the leaders of Croatia and Slovenia that they couldn't remain partnered with the Serbs—or, at the very least, Milosevic gave them a pretext for stoking their own nationalisms. Croatia and Slovenia moved toward declaring their own independent states, declarations Serbia countered with war.

Romantic trappings of war could be found everywhere. The media railed against the Croatian treatment of its Serb minority, a story that tugged at the heart strings of the nation. But Serbia didn't have enough men in its army willing to go off and do the dirty work. Draft dodging became a rite of passage. My translator described to me how he faked insanity and created pus-filled infections on his face to end his service after fifty-two days. Young men slept in different apartments each night, hoping to evade the conscriptors. At one desperate point, police began pulling men from restaurants in Belgrade and shipping them to the front. In addition to the problem of the rank and file, there was the problem of the brass. The army's high command had emerged from a military culture steeped in communism. They had been trained to believe in an even-handed Yugoslavian state arbitrating between the ethnicities.

Without a reliable regular army, the Serb leaders began to discreetly compile paramilitary forces. Arkan's Delije proved an irresistible recruiting vehicle. The Delije, after all, had a reputation for inflicting cruel violence and then celebrating it in their songs ("Axes in hand/and a knife in the teeth/there'll be blood tonight"). Under Arkan, they were now operating within a carefully delineated hierarchy that responded to the commands of a single leader. And as they proved against Dinamo Zagreb in the famous televised match, they actually enjoyed fighting Croats. The government preferred this hooligan style. Serbia didn't need conventional troops to fight another army. Very little of that sort of combat actually took place in the Balkans. The government needed a force that could terrorize civilians, causing Muslims and Croats to flee their homes in the territories that the Serbs hoped to control.

In Yugoslav papers—and for that matter across the world—war had been a metaphor for sports. Teams would battle and attack; they had impenetrable defenses and strikers who fired volleys. Now, Arkan's men brought the metaphor to life. As he put it in an interview a few years later, "We fans first trained without weapons. . . . Since our first beginning I insisted on discipline. Fans make noise, they want to get drunk, fool around. I decided to stop all this with one blow; I made them cut their hair, shave regularly, stop drinking, and everything went on track."

Arkan called his army the Tigers, but they might as well have been called the Delije. Recruits from Red Star trained at a government-supplied police base in the Croatian town of Erdut. They were, by all accounts, armed to the hilt. Writing in a Belgrade sports paper in 1992, a reporter filed a dispatch on the Tigers: "I wind back the film of my memories and distribute these brave boys through all the stadiums of Europe. I know exactly where each of them stood, who first started the song, who unfurled his flag, who lit the first torch. The Delije have left their supporters' props somewhere under the arches of Marakana stadium and have set off to the war with rifles in their hands."

But they hadn't left all their fan behavior behind. The Belgrade anthropologist Ivan Colovic has shown that the fans took their stadium songs with them to the front. They tinkered with the lyrics ever so slightly to place them clearly into military context. Red Star players would drive to Arkan's camp to visit wounded fans. Red Star's captain Vladan Lukic told the *Serbian Journal*, "Many of our loyal supporters from the north end of Marakana [stadium] are in the most obvious ways writing the finest pages of the history of Serbia."

III.

Arkan's army fought in the first Serb offensive of 1991–92 and immediately began to earn its notorious reputation. Pictures of Arkan's exploits turned the West decisively against Serbia. Most famously, there were the stomach-churning photographs from Bijeljina. In one, Arkan kisses the president of the Bosnian Serb Republic while standing over the corpse of a Muslim civilian. Others showed Tigers kicking lifeless bodies and stepping on the skulls of their victims.

When Croatia launched a well-armed counteroffensive in 1995, Arkan remobilized his army. He watched the Croats reconquer territory on the television in his home across from Red Star's stadium. As his wife recounted the story to me, the images made him violently angry. "They are killing my people. I need to go to war," he exclaimed. At the time, Arkan had only been married a few weeks. His wife says that she appealed to his sense of marital obligation. "You've got a family to think of now," she told him. Instead of rebutting her, he silently retreated to their bedroom. Ten minutes later, when she went to check on him, she found him dressed in his fatigues and beret. Within thirty minutes, after one phone call, his army had assembled in front of the Red Star stadium.

Arkan waged some of his bloodiest offensives near the Bosnian town of Sasina. To oversee his operations, he set up a command post in the manager's office of the Hotel Sanus. From there, he sent the Tigers on patrols to detain Muslim men, evict their families, and loot their homes. Theft had become a prime goal of the

Tigers. One witness told the *Los Angeles Times,* "When they entered a cleansed Muslim house, a couple of them would head for the kitchen and start moving out kitchen appliances. Others would go for the television and the VCR. Somebody else would start digging in the garden, looking for buried jewelry. You could always recognize Arkan's men. They had dirty fingernails from digging." As the Tigers captured Muslims in Sasina, they transported them to Arkan's hotel headquarters. Some were beaten and interrogated. Others were crammed into a basement boiler room, five square meters in size. For more than three days, the Tigers kept thirty men and one woman in this space, without food, water, or adequate ventilation. A bus transported detainees from the boiler room to the foot of a hill looking up at a village church. They killed all but two of the detainees, shoving them into mass graves that would be exhumed a year later. By the end of the war in Croatia and Bosnia, according to State Department estimates, with throat slitting, strangulation, and other forms of execution, Arkan's Tigers had killed at least 2,000 men and women.

Arkan's crimes had been documented well. In Serbian society, it wasn't hard to find out about them. Milosevic hadn't curtailed access to the Internet, hadn't banned satellite dishes, hadn't tossed out the human rights activists. The Belgrade dissident Filip David told me quite simply, "We knew." But instead of greeting Arkan with moral opprobrium, Serbian society turned him into a hero.

Many of the Serbs who watched Arkan's veneration, now compare it to the laudatory, fascinated coverage that Americans devoted to John Gotti and Al Capone. This comparison, however, understates both Arkan's wickedness and the swooning of the Serb press. With regular appearances on the wildly popular *Minimaxovision* variety show, Arkan presented himself as a charming persona that even the country's middle class could adore. He used these cameos to announce his marriage to the pop star Ceca and the impending births of their children. When he married Ceca in 1994, TV carried the event live.

The war hadn't just made Arkan famous; it made him rich, too. Patriotism had provided the justification for looting on a grand scale. Arkan ran his network, the Tigers, as a black market sanctions-busting conglomerate, cornering monopolies on petroleum and consumer goods. Some in Belgrade jokingly dubbed the city's shopping districts "Arkansas." Here, the American gangster metaphor really does work. Like many Mafiosos before him, Arkan was intent on parlaying this newfangled wealth into legitimacy. More specifically, he hoped to become the president of a championship soccer club that would provide him with international prestige and even more adoration. When Red Star wouldn't sell the club to him, Arkan set out to create his own Red Star. First, he bought a team in Kosovo and purged its largely ethnic Albanian lineup. Then, in 1996 he traded up for the Belgrade club Obilic, a semi-professional team that had lingered in Yugoslavia's lower divisions for decades.

Part of Obilic's appeal was its namesake, a knight who fought at the Serbs' defeat in the 1389 battle for Kosovo—the defining moment in the national narrative of victimization. Just before the battle, Obilic infiltrated the Turkish camp and stabbed the Sultan Murad with a poisoned dagger. Arkan added to this preexisting mystique, figuring himself a latter-day Obilic. He changed the color of the club's uniform to yellow, a tribute to his Tigers, and made the tiger a ubiquitous symbol spread through the stadium. Its face greets you as you enter the club's headquarters. It appears on the doors of vehicles the club owns.

Almost instantly, under Arkan's stewardship, the club triumphed. Within a year of arriving in the top division, it won the national championship. Arkan liked to brag about the secrets of his success; the fact that he paid his players the highest salaries in the country; that he forbade them to drink before games; that he disciplined his players to act as a military unit. But his opponents provide another explanation for Obilic's impossibly rapid ascent. According to one widely reported account, Arkan had threatened to shoot a rival striker's kneecap if he scored against Obilic. Another player told the English soccer magazine *Four-Four-Two* that he'd been locked in a garage while his team played against Obilic.

At games, Arkan's message to his opponents was clear enough. Obilic's corps of supporters consisted substantially of veteran paramilitaries. These Tigers would "escort" referees to the game in their jeeps. At games, they would chant things like "If you score, you'll never walk out of the stadium alive" or "We'll break both your legs, you'll walk on your hands." As English newspapers pointed out, it was in the player's best interest to adhere to the demands. Fans were frequently waving guns at them.

According to Belgrade lore, Arkan made a habit of barging into opposing teams' locker rooms during half time, where he would shout abuse. To avoid this fate, Red Star once simply refused to leave the field during the game break. Its players loitered on the pitch, even urinated on the side of field, rather than risk encountering Arkan. After another match, Red Star Belgrade striker Perica Ognjenovic complained, "This is not soccer, this is war. I think I'd better leave this country."

With its overnight success, Obilic had qualified to compete against other top teams in the European Champions League. But even the European soccer officials—not exactly sticklers when it comes to criminals and dictators—couldn't tolerate the presence of Arkan at their stadiums. They banned the club from continental competition. To get around the ban, Arkan resigned from the club. He installed his wife, Ceca, as his replacement. It didn't take a prosecutor from The Hague to poke holes in this sleight of hand. When I interviewed Ceca, she told me, "I was the president. He was the advisor." She chuckled at the mention of both president and advisor.

Obilic never flourished in continental competition. Arkan hadn't dared lock players from Bayern Munich and other giant European clubs in garages. Soon, Obilic began to slip in the domestic game, too. After Obilic's championship season, clubs understood that throwing the championship to Arkan had exacted too great a financial cost. They banded together and dared Arkan to kill them all. "The teams called one another and said, 'We can't let this happen again,' " the theater director and soccer columnist Gorcin Stojanovic told me. With the clubs aligned against him, Arkan deployed intimidation less frequently. Obilic began to fade into the middle of the league table.

In the end, Obilic may have been Arkan's undoing. There are many theories to explain why in January 2000 he was gunned down in the lobby of the Intercontinental Hotel, where he liked to take his morning coffee and use the gym. One holds that Milosevic's son Marko had resented the monopoly that Arkan possessed on the black market. Another holds that the secret police needed to eliminate Arkan. He knew too much and could be too easily lured to The Hague to testify against Milosevic. Or perhaps it was simply a gangland battle over turf. There is, however, another explanation, one that I favor for its poetic justice. Obilic might have been the proximate cause of his death. His partners had resented that he took such a large share of the profits from the sale of players; they felt that they could no longer do business with him. After he exploited soccer to destroy lives, soccer would now destroy his own.

IV.

There had always been a small, liberal anti-Milosevic opposition within Belgrade. Around the time of Arkan's death, their moment finally arrived. Hardship had brought Serbs to an epiphany: What had a decade of warfare achieved, except international isolation and stupendous inflation? To jump-start the anti-Milosevic movement, the liberal leaders called in two groups to provide bodies for demonstrations, the student union and Red Star's Delije. Ever since the late eighties, Milosevic had worried that the Delije's sincere attachment to Serbian nationalism might stand in the way of his cynical machinations. Now, the Delije rose to obstruct him.

Red Star fans like to say that they were the agents of political change. Indeed, the guys at the front of the barricades and the ones who stormed government buildings in search of evidence proving Milosevic's corruption wore replica Red Star jerseys. They would leave games to fight with police near Milosevic's villa. There, Delije members like Krle and Draza shouted for opposition politicians to "Save Serbia from this mad house." At games, they sang, "Kill yourself, Slobodan." To prevent protests, at one point, Milosevic's regime allegedly began buying up tickets to national team matches and distributing them to friendly faces.

Serbs have placed Milosevic's overthrow in 2000— the Red Star Revolution, let's call it—in the pantheon of great anticommunist revolts. They see it as the conclusion to the Velvet Revolution that began in 1989. But had this revolt changed a nation, with anything like the transformative effect of Havel's ascent to the Prague castle, or Walesa's presidency? For a revolt to change a nation, the Serbs wouldn't just have to pull down the iconography of the dictator Milosevic, as the Russians had knocked over the figures of Lenin. They would have had to topple Arkan, the wicked id of the country, from his central place in the culture.

When I visited Belgrade, Arkan's image remained upright. Two years after the Red Star Revolution, and three years after his death, he still haunted the streets of Belgrade. At newsstands, his mug gleamed on the glossy covers of big-selling tabloids. In bookstalls, he stared heroically from dust jackets. Notices fixed to lampposts advertised a kickboxing match held in the commandant's memory.

Obilic exists as the greatest monument to the man. Its stadium may be the most thoroughly modern building in Belgrade, with swooping steel, glass, and a row of plush executive suites. Arkan's old office overlooks the field from the top of an adjoining tower. By post-communist standards, it's a remarkable room. Marble and Persian rugs cover the floors. On top of a wooden bookshelf, a framed photo lovingly captures the warlord in his battle garb. The room's massive wooden desk displays a bronze statue of Arkan with Obilic's championship medals draped from his neck. In a far corner, a collection of swords pays homage to the warrior Obilic as does a canvas-and-oil portrait of the medieval swain. On a shelf, in plain sight, a box advertises itself as containing a laser-guide for a pistol.

In Arkan's old office, I'd been granted an audience with his widow, the pop idol Ceca, the woman he had married on national television. She entered the room smoking a cigarette. Everyone had told me about her body. Now I understood what they meant. Her shiny green blouse failed to contain her enormous, silicone-filled breasts. This was not an unusual flaunting. Ceca won international renown for standing on the sidelines during Obilic matches in skintight leopard print outfits. She sat across from me on a leather couch. Before the meeting, my translator cautioned me to tread carefully.

Arkan's family, he said, still had access to Arkan's
henchmen. I was not inclined to push the envelope that
far. Besides, it wouldn't have gotten me anywhere.
From her experiences traveling in Europe with Obilic,
she acquired savvy about Western journalists. She
understood the need to puncture the aura of war crimi-
nality. "It's horrible to make connections between politics and sports. I condemn any effort to turn the game
into politics," she said with a look of earnest disgust.
Over and over, she repeated, "This is a business, a
game. Nothing more."

With her banality, it became easy to forget her evil.
But she had a long history of dabbling in extremist politics. During the war, she played benefit concerts for
Arkan's ultranationalist political party. "You can be
happy as me—just join the Serbian Unity Party," she
would announce to her many adoring fans. As the Serbian Unity Party's Web site describes, she continues to
fund a campaign to defend the Serb nation against the
"white plague" of "non-Serb nationalities." Even without Arkan, his party is run from her home. Last summer, she performed a concert at Red Star stadium,
dedicated to Arkan, where she led 100,000 fans in
chanting his name.

But with her homespun charms and kitschy dance
music, called "turbo-folk," she succeeds wildly in ful-
filling both parts of Hannah Arendt's famous phrase
about the banality of evil. "I'm the team mama," she
says. "That's how they think of me. I want my players
to look the best, so I give them Armani." She describes
a forthcoming trip to the NBA All Star game in Atlanta
and speaks of the pleasures of decorating Arkan's office.

Under Ceca's presidency, since Arkan's death, Obilic hasn't had much luck. This is strangely fitting. The club really only existed as a tribute to the man— and what he represented. After I interviewed Ceca, she invited me to visit the club's museum. Obilic's top executive, a retired player, led me around the room. He showed me medals and photos. But the heart of the exhibit was a wall of photos that documented Arkan's revival of Obilic's fortunes. My tour guide pointed proudly and said, "Our father."

Serbia's prime minister Zoran Djindjic frequently played soccer. In part, he played out of genuine enthusiasm for the game. In part, he liked the image that the game created, of youthful vigor. Elected in 2000, Djindjic sold himself to the country as the reformer who would reverse the damages wrought by the Milosevic regime. This was a program that necessarily put him on a collision course with organized crime, the bureaucracy, and the mafia-linked security services. It made him despised by the Serbian people, who hated his anti-inflationary policies and his close relations with the same European and American governments that had bombed Belgrade. With the political deck so stacked against him, Djindjic needed every Kennedyesque image he could get.

Early in March of 2003, Djindjic played in a match between a government team and police officers. He arrived unannounced. Surprised police officers didn't know how to play against a prime minister. Should they throw him the match or play extra hard so that they could later brag about beating the most powerful Serb? They must have decided that they would tackle him as hard as any opponent. In the match, the prime minister injured his Achilles tendon. For the next few weeks, he hobbled around on crutches. At lunchtime on March 12, he exited his car and began to move slowly toward a government office building. A man masquerading as a maintenance worker trained a Heckler & Koch G3 gun on the prime minister. A bullet pushed Djindjic's heart from his body.

The Djindjic assassination shocked Serbia into carrying out part of the Djindjic program. Outraged and mournful, the public finally got behind his plans for cleaning up organized crime. Police rounded up as many gangsters and their fellow travelers as they could find. Five days into this purge, they arrived at Ceca's house across from the Red Star stadium and placed her under arrest. They had come after her because she had met frequently with suspected accomplices in the murder, including rendezvous before *and* after the dastardly deed.

When police arrived, they found a door to a secret bunker beneath Ceca's palace. It took several hours to break through the entrance, but when they did, they found quite a cache, dozens of guns, thousands of rounds of ammunition, silencers, and laser guides, just like the one I had seen on the shelf in her office. The police locked Ceca in solitary confinement and left her there for a month. In the meantime, they began scouring her finances, especially related to Obilic, and found that there had barely been the pretense of legality in the operation. After selling her players, Ceca would allegedly stuff the profits into her personal accounts in Cyprus and Hungary.

To be sure, Serbia hadn't fully taken on its problem. Nobody particularly questioned the ideology of Serb nationalism, the idea that Serbs possess a morality and character superior to their non-Serb neighbors. Nobody questioned the idea of the Serbs' eternal victimhood. In fact, the Djindjic assassination was cast as another instance of history screwing them. And, of course, the Ultra Bad Boys of Red Star continued to be ultra bad. But, finally, there were subtle signs of discomfort with the national culture of gangsterism.

Ceca tried many stunts to yank the public into her corner, but none really worked. A hunger strike ended quickly after it began. When her friends held a rally on her thirtieth birthday, only 1,500 loyalists showed—a far cry from the 100,000 that attended her last concert in the Red Star stadium. Ultimately, a court ruled her incarceration unconstitutional, after she had spent four months behind bars. But for once, in Serbia, evil shed its coat of banality and could be identified as itself.

2

How Soccer Explains
the Pornography of Sects

I.

In full throat, they sing in praise of our slaughter. *We're up to our knees in Fenian blood.* There are 44,000 of them, mostly Protestant supporters of the Glasgow Rangers Football Club. As this is their home stadium, Ibrox, they can make their songs as virulent as they please. *If you hate the fuckin' Fenians clap your hands.* We, the 7,000 supporters of Glasgow's traditionally Catholic Celtic Football Club, sit in a separate section of the stadium allocated to visitors, behind the goal. *Surrender or you'll die.* Although surveillance cameras track every move in Ibrox, it feels as if only a line of policemen in yellow slickers stands as a barricade blocking the home crowd from making good on its songs. *With a rifle or a pistol in my hand.*

Outside the stadium, thirty minutes to game time, a crowd of Rangers supporters makes a move toward the

visitors' entrance. When police on horseback halt their
progress, they extend their arms forward in a stiff
salute and belt "Rule Britannia," the anthem of the
empire. It goes without saying, they believe that Britannia should rule the Celtic stock of Irish Catholics. Compared to the rest of their gestures and songs, this hardly
offends. Scattered across the stands, Rangers fans wear
orange shirts and hold orange banners to commemo-
rate the ejection of the Catholic monarchy in 1688 by
William of Orange, or "King Billy" as they call him.
King Billy's modern-day heirs receive their dues as well.
Encomiums to the Ulster Volunteer Force and Ulster
Defense Association, the Protestant paramilitaries in
Northern Ireland, have been stitched into scarves and
written into songs. When Rangers sing, "Hello, hello,
we are the Billy Boys," they are associating themselves
with a gang that rampaged against Glasgow's Catholics
between the wars. In the 1920s, the Billy Boys estab-
lished the local affiliate of the Ku Klux Klan.

Matches between cross-town rivals always make for
the most combustible dates on the schedule. These
rivalries generate the game's horror stories: jobs denied
because of allegiance to the foe; fans murdered for
wearing the wrong jersey in the wrong neighborhood.
Nobody, it seems, hates like a neighbor. But the Celtic-
Rangers rivalry represents something more than the
enmity of proximity. It is an unfinished fight over the
Protestant Reformation.

Some of the consequences of the Celtic-Rangers
derby can be tabulated. According to an activist group
that monitors Glasgow's sectarianism, during such
weekends, admissions in the city's emergency wards

increase nine-fold. Over the last seven years, the match has run up a toll of eight directly related deaths in Glasgow. In the two and a half hours following a match in May 1999, the police blotter recorded these crimes committed by Rangers fans in their saturnalia:

> Karl McGraorty, twenty years old, shot in the chest with a crossbow leaving a Celtic pub.
> Liam Sweeney, twenty-five years old, in a green shirt, beaten by four assailants in a Chinese carryout.
> Thomas McFadden, sixteen years of age, stabbed in the chest, stomach, and groin—killed after watching the game in an Irish pub.

In the stadium, the intensity can be gauged without numbers. Across the police line, a pimply pubescent with red hair and an orange jersey furiously thrusts a poster-size Union Jack with his hands. Like winter breath, the bile blows from his mouth. When he screams— *Up to our knees in Fenian blood*—I'm quite sure that he means it. Right next to him, a man who must be his father sings along.

All this in Glasgow, the city that nurtured Adam Smith, Francis Hutcheson, and the no-nonsense northern wing of the Enlightenment. A bit more than one hundred years later, Charles Rennie Mackintosh gave its downtown a singular, modern architectural vernacular. Even when Glasgow hit the post-industrial economic skids, it didn't turn reactionary. Its polity aligned itself with liberal yuppie Britain in the Labour coalition. On

Buchanan Street, with the commercial bustle, unavoidable Starbucks, prosperous immigrant merchants, and overwhelming modernist concert hall at its head, it's possible to believe that you're standing at the urbane intersection where, as the political theorist Frances Fukuyama imagined it, history ends.

According to most schools of social science, places like Glasgow were supposed to have conquered ancient tribalism. This was the theory of modernization, handed down from Karl Marx, refined in the sixties by academics like Daniel Bell, enshrined in the foreign policy of the United States government, and rehashed by the globalization enthusiasts of the nineties. It posited that once a society becomes economically advanced, it would become politically advanced—liberal, tolerant, democratic. Sure, tinges of racism would continue to exist in its working classes, and it could be hard to transcend poverty, but that's why social safety nets existed. When the globalization theorists of the nineties posited the thesis, they added that business was supposed to play a part in this triumph of tolerance. Everyone would assimilate into a homogenizing mass entertainment culture, where TV comedies and cinematic romances bind together different races into a new union of common pop references. And to attain the ultimate prize of global reach, business would exude multiculturalism— "the United Colors of. . . ."

Indeed, the Celtic and Rangers organizations want to convert themselves into international capitalist entities and entertainment conglomerates. They understand that they have to become something more than adversaries in a centuries-old religious war. Graeme

Souness, a manager of Rangers in the late eighties and early nineties, explained that his club faced a choice between "success and sectarianism." At the time, he believed that his organization had opted for the former. Like Celtic's management, Rangers have done everything possible to move beyond the relatively small Scottish market—sending clothing catalogues to the Scottish and Irish diasporas in North America; campaigning to move from the Scottish Premier League to the bigger, wealthier English League.

At the game's end, on the field, these capitalist aspirations are plenty apparent. As the Protestants celebrate a goal, they're egged on by the team captain, a long-haired Italian called Lorenzo Amoruso, who has the look of a 1980s male model. Flailing his arms, he urges them to sing their anti-Catholic songs louder. The irony is obvious: Amoruso is a Catholic. For that matter, so are most of the Rangers players. Since the late nineties, Rangers routinely field nearly as many Catholics as Celtic. Their players come from Georgia, Argentina, Germany, Sweden, Portugal, and Holland, because money can buy no better ones. Championships mean more than religious purity.

For all their capitalist goals, however, Rangers don't try too hard to discourage religious bigotry. They continue to hawk orange jerseys. They play songs on the Ibrox loudspeaker that they know will provoke anti-Catholic lyrics: Tina Turner's "Simply the Best" culminates in 40,000 screams of "Fuck the pope!" The clubs stoke ethnic hatred, or make only periodic attempts to discourage it, because they know ethnic hatred makes good business sense. Even in the global market, they draw supporters who crave ethnic identification—to join an existential fight on behalf of their tribe. If they lost their extremist sloganeering, they'd lose money. In fact, from the start of their rivalry, Celtic and Rangers have been nicknamed the "Old Firm," because they're seen as colluding to profit from their mutual hatreds.

Of course, the modernization thesis provides plenty of explanations for illiberal hatreds—competition for scarce jobs, an inadequate welfare state—but none of those conditions exists in any great concentration in Glasgow. Discrimination has faded. Its unemployment problem is now no better or worse than the rest of Britain. The city has kept alive its soccer tribalism, despite the logic of history, because it provides the city with a kind of pornographic pleasure.

II.

The night before the Old Firm match, I have drinks at the Grapes pub, an epicenter of Rangers fandom on the south bank of the Clyde River. Picture postcards of Queen Elizabeth have been strung in a row and hang over the bar. Union Jacks cover most surfaces on the wall not occupied by framed photos of Rangers players. The exterior has been pointedly painted a royalist blue. Outsiders who enter the pub are looked upon as potential Celtic infiltrators. To ease my assimilation at the Grapes, I have a friend call a regular who vouches for me with the clientele. My connection doesn't help with some of the drunks. They laugh when I introduce myself as Frank. "That's not short for Francis?" one asks. "You aren't a Tim, are ya?" And nobody especially wants to talk to a journalist, who I'm sure they suspect will lampoon them for their deeply held beliefs. After a while, I give up and sit at the bar, staring at a drunk making clumsy passes at the only two women in the room. That's when a man called Dummy drapes his arm around me and blows his whiskey breath in my ear. "In 1979," he says, "I spent sixteen hours getting pissed in a bar outside Buffalo."

Dummy introduces himself as James, but announces that he prefers to go by his nickname. It conveys recklessness, he says, and recklessness is a prime characteristic of movie mobsters. From the start, Dummy makes a big point of establishing his hard man bona fides. He shows me two fresh knife scars on his face from pub brawls over money owed to him— "just from the last six months," he claims. But those fights were atavistic. Dummy's career as a hard man is in the past. He's over forty now, with a wizened face, a wife, teenage children, and a legitimate business. In fact, he says that he has become rich from his firm, which deploys scaffolding to building sites.

Dummy comes from the west coast of Scotland but lives in an English factory town, several hours from Glasgow by car. His father had moved the family south to follow the migration of industry in the 1960s. He took with him his intense Scottish pride and his love of Rangers. Although he couldn't indoctrinate Dummy's siblings, Dummy bit hard. Dummy dreams of retiring to Glasgow one day. "It's not Florida, okay," he says, pressing his belly into the bar, trying to grab the bartender's attention. "This is the greatest place on the planet. The water tastes better. The people aren't English. Top quality people, here."

Dummy makes it his mission to convert me to the Rangers cause. "There's no way that you, a smart man, especially a smart American, will come away from this game without loving Glasgow Rangers. Celtic are terrorists. Listen to all the songs about the IRA. After eleventh of September, how can they do that?" Because he's bought me two glasses of cheap house scotch, his arguments make a measure of sense. But Dummy's biggest selling point is the medium of his message, not the substance; he has a life-consuming passion for his team. He points in the direction of his Rangers boxer shorts. "I love Rangers football club. If I had to choose between my job and Rangers, I'd choose Rangers. If I had to choose between my wife and Rangers, I'd choose Rangers." Indeed, about sixteen weekends a year, he chooses Rangers over his wife, gathering his mates, drinking two tall glasses of whiskey for the road, putting sectarian tunes into the car sound system, and making the long drive north.

Among soccer fans, there's a continuum of hooliganism. On one extreme exist true thugs like the notorious supporters of such British clubs as Millwall and Cardiff City. Although they'll profess love of club, beating the shit out of people (including fellow fans) is their telos. Those kinds of thugs, however, are few and far between, and many have been priced out of attending games in bigger cities like Glasgow, Manchester, and London. Next, quite a few steps closer to sanity, there's a vast lumpen proletariat. Where the thugs are often organized into marauding "firms," the lumpen proletariat belongs to benign supporters clubs, meeting for pints and traveling to games together in chartered coaches. They are not innately violent men. They hold down good jobs and have loving families. But like much of Britain, when vast quantities of lager courses through them they can become a bit brutish. On weekends, they find themselves screaming at a cab driver who supports Celtic, or getting into a scuffle outside the Celtic bar down the block. Dummy is an avatar of this vast lumpen proletariat.

There's a tendency to caricature the feelings of soccer fans like Dummy. These men are often depicted as dupes of jingoistic politicians, driven to hatred by ignorance or economic resentment or just deep-seated inferiority. But it's hard to detect any of these qualities in Rangers fans. In fact, far from sounding like ignoramuses, they possess remarkable historical literacy. Describing his love of Rangers, Dummy provides a cogent narrative of Scottish Protestantism: "In 1646 at Portadown. . . ." Off the top of his head, even in his sotted state, he spews dozens of important dates.

As Dummy points out, the story of Celtic and Rangers traces back to the sixeenth century. The Protestant reformation sank its talons into Scotland with greater ferocity than anywhere else in Europe. When John Knox's disciples spread north from their bases in Glasgow and Edinburgh, they violently stamped out Catholic strongholds, resorting to ethnic cleansing in a few cases. Their theocracy executed Edinburgh students for casually doubting the existence of the Lord—and purged society of most hints of papistry. By the end of the eighteenth century, Glasgow possessed thirty-nine Catholics and forty-three anti-Catholic societies.

Three hundred years into the reformation, however, Catholics began to reappear in their midst in a major way. With potato blight making life across the Irish Sea untenable, thousands of immigrants escaped to Glasgow seeking relief. They'd been among the poorest, least educated émigrés—the ones who couldn't afford tickets to Boston and New York. Dazed by their new home and excluded from the rest of society, they had little choice but to stick mostly to themselves. A structure of virtual apartheid evolved. Glasgow's Catholics attended separate schools. Shut out of Protestant professional firms, Catholics started their own. And in 1888, a Marist monk named Father Walfrid began the community's own soccer club, Celtic.

Walfrid created Celtic out of fear. By the late nineteenth century, Catholics had good reasons to worry about the influence of Protestant missionaries, whose wealth and soup kitchens allowed them to evangelize in the Catholic strongholds. Leisure time of Catholic youth needed to be filled by Catholic institutions, or else Protestant ones would claim the void. A winning football club, Walfrid also hoped, could puncture the myth of Catholic inferiority. Indeed, Celtic succeeded wildly. Because it played with something to prove, Celtic soon captured four of six league championships.

Protestant Scotland didn't passively accept Celtic's success. The soccer press put out the call for a "Scottish" team to retake the championship. Rangers began with no particular religious or political aspirations. But when it racked up wins against Celtic, Protestant Scotland imposed religious and political aspirations upon the club and gradually adopted Rangers as its own.

The Old Firm hadn't started as an especially violent affair, but it quickly became one. During the first two decades of the twentieth century, ethnic hatred in Glasgow ratcheted up. The Harland and Wolff Shipbuilding Company, a Protestant firm, relocated from Belfast, bringing with it thousands of Protestant workers and their expertise in despising Catholics. The new yard, however, couldn't compensate for the woes of Glasgow shipbuilding. In the 1920s, as German and American industry surged, Scotland felt the Great Depression ten years earlier than anyone else. With intense competition for limited jobs, the inevitable religious scapegoating kicked in, and the Church of Scotland began grousing about the Irish menace. That's when the Old Firm first turned poisonous. The Billy Boys gang of Rangers thugs, along with Celtic equivalents like McGrory Boys and McGlynn Push, fought one another with guns, knives, and no restraint.

The press likes to describe Celtic and Rangers as moral equals. And it's true that Celtic has used its stadium for open-air celebration of mass; chunks of its management devotedly backed the Irish republican cause; and its directors consisted exclusively of Catholics up through the 1990s. There was, however, a substantial gulf between the practices of the two clubs. Celtic made an early calculation to field non-Catholics in their green and white jerseys; Rangers did no similar thing. Sometime in the vicinity of World War I, Rangers instituted a Protestants-only policy, extending from players to janitors. And it became even more stringent than that: The club denied promotions to executives who *married* Catholics. Rangers allowed itself to become a staging ground for strident Protestant politics. It sent teams to Belfast for benefit matches, with proceeds going to Northern Irish chapters of the Orange Order—the anti-Catholic fraternal organization that seems to exist for no other reason than ominously marching through Catholic neighborhoods on July twelfth, the anniversary of King Billy's 1690 triumph at the Battle of Boyne. Ibrox Stadium became the citywide focal point for Glasgow's own July twelfth celebrations. One of the club's official histories describes its ethos bluntly enough: "a Protestant club for Protestant people."

Considering postwar history—decolonization, civil rights, a global push toward liberalization—Rangers stubbornly held back until late in the program. Perhaps it was appropriate that Rangers tore down its religious wall in 1989, the year of the Velvet Revolution. The club's new president, David Murray, prodded by his manager Graeme Souness, signed an ex-Celtic Catholic named Maurice Johnston. (Actually, Johnston's father was a Protestant Rangers fan and he never really practiced Catholicism himself.) Even then, Rangers weren't pushed into their decision by do-gooders. It was purely a business decision. During the 1980s, enticed by rising television revenues, a new generation of capitalists entered the game to make some real money, a breed far more sophisticated than the amateur rogues and philanthropically minded bourgeoisie who'd ruled before. David Murray, for one, had made his fortune as a steel magnate. Although he hardly preached progressive politics, he understood that sectarianism had become a potential financial drag. The European soccer federation, he feared, would impose costly sanctions on Rangers if it didn't alter its hiring. He also understood that relying exclusively on Protestants had deprived Rangers of the talent to compete at the highest European levels, where top clubs like Real Madrid and AC Milan had imported Latin American stars as Catholic as they come.

Rather predictably, the Catholic acquisition didn't go down easy among the faithful. Fans gathered outside Ibrox to set fire to Rangers scarves and seasons tickets. They laid wreaths to mourn the passing of the club's Protestant identity. In Northern Ireland, supporters clubs passed resolutions banning travel to Glasgow for games and boycotting the purchase of Rangers products. Effigies of Graeme Souness burned in Belfast streets.

By becoming the Jackie Robinson of Scottish soccer, Johnston put his own life in jeopardy. Celtic fans staged their own protests, denouncing him as a turncoat. They sprayed graffiti threatening, "Collaborators Can't Play Without Kneecaps." For a while, it looked as though the authors of that phrase—or their sympathizers—might turn the threat into reality. A month after Johnston's arrival, police detained Celtic fans who had allegedly plotted to assassinate him. To keep their new purchase alive, Rangers shipped him from Glasgow to London each night on a chartered jet; Johnston later moved into a safe-house outside Edinburgh. By the mid-nineties, he fled Scotland altogether, resettling in the friendlier confines of Kansas City.

Jackie Robinson's presence transformed the culture of

baseball, slowly chipping away at clubhouse racism. Mo Johnston, strangely, had the opposite effect. The team began to travel with a picture of the Queen that it hung in the dressing rooms it visited. Players began to appear in Northern Ireland, photographed alongside paramilitaries. Scottish Protestant players allegedly defecated all over the Celtic changing room when Rangers borrowed it for a match. Even Mo Johnston himself was witnessed singing the "Sash," a ballad with anti-Catholic inflections. And Rangers's growing contingent of Catholics followed his lead in singing songs that insulted their faith.

How to explain this strange inversion? Glasgow is not an enormous city. Average people regularly encounter their soccer heroes. They run into them in the pubs and on the streets. If the players aren't appropriately enthusiastic about the cause, their lives can become very difficult. They already have to contend with half the town hating them; they don't need their own fans turning on them, too. It creates a feedback loop that ensures sectarianism's persistence. When Graeme Souness left the club in 1991, he told a press conference, "Bigotry never sat easily on my shoulders, and bigotry will always be at Ibrox." With Dummy whispering into my ear—"I'll never hire a Celtic supporter"—I think I know what he means.

III.

The next day, as I leave my hotel for the stadium, the staff tries to give me advice. Most of them had never been to a Celtic-Rangers game, despite the importance of the event in the life of the city. Still, they felt a sense of civic pride, constantly assuring me of my safety at Ibrox. As I departed, a receptionist rose from her chair. "You'll have a fantastic time," she said, suddenly stopping me. "Hold on. Open your jacket." A few days earlier, I'd told her that I suffer from a very mild red-green colorblindness. Now, she wanted to proofread my clothes to make sure that I had filtered out all royalist blue, Ulster orange, and Irish green that might incite a drunken thug. Every sane Glaswegian had told me to advertise my neutrality as clearly as possible. "Wear black," one friend advised. Before the receptionist's intervention, I'd already set aside sweaters whose hues I didn't want to risk. The receptionist laughed at herself for conducting this examination, "You'll be fine. Just remember, whatever you hear, they don't really mean it."

Everything I do at the game to register my noncombatant status seems to fail. Although I introduce myself as an American writer on a research mission, my neighbors in the Celtic stands insist on partisanship. Frank, the roofer in the seat next to mine, tries to explain the atmosphere by pointing to the field and intoning, "Good versus evil." Another neighbor wraps a "Fighting Irish" scarf around my neck. He hoists my arms in the air above my head, a reverent gesture, during the singing of the Rodgers and Hammerstein ballad "You'll Never Walk Alone."

After Celtic score a goal twenty seconds into the game, a stranger's embrace lifts me above my seat. My cell phone tumbles out of my pocket, two rows down. Our section turns to the Rangers fans and sings about the exploits of the IRA. I don't know the words, and can't always cut through the brogues to decipher them, but there are certain phrases that are easy enough to pick up. *Fuck the Queen. Orange Bastards.* Frank the roofer translates for me, until he explains that the vulgarity makes him feel ashamed.

Spurred on by the home fans, Rangers players exude the dour Calvinism that they are supposed to represent. They tackle hard and neglect no defensive detail. Their midfielders slide into Celtic's. Their effort yields a string of three unanswered goals. When the Protestants sing "shit Fenian bastards," we have no response other than to extend our middle fingers and use them as batons to ironically conduct their taunts.

Rangers wins the match three-two, and there's only one explanation for the outcome: Celtic's sluggish and sloppy back line of defense. That fact doesn't interfere with the explanations I overhear for the defeat. "Give a goddam Orangeman a whistle. . . ." Another man refers to referees as the "masons in black." Of course, grousing about refereeing is a bedrock right of sports fans. Why blame the team that you love when culpability for defeats can be easily transported elsewhere?

Celtic fans are a special case. They don't just believe that referees try to ruin them. They believe that they've definitively proved the phenomenon. The case against the "masons in black" has been made on the op-ed pages of broadsheets and in the pages of the Glasgow archdiocese's newspaper, and, most elaborately, by a Jesuit priest called Peter Burns. Basing his study on several decades' worth of game accounts in the *Glasgow Herald*, Father Burns found that referees had disallowed sixteen Celtic goals, while denying Rangers a mere four. Celtic had won two "dubious penalties" to Rangers' eight. "It seems reasonable to conclude," he wrote, adopting the tone of a disinterested academic, "that the oft-made and oft-denied charge of Rangers-favoring bias by match officials, at least in Old Firm games, does indeed stand up to scrutiny." When Celtic supporters make their case, they invariably point to a string of incidents. First, they point to a passage in the memoir of a Rangers player recounting a retired referee bragging to him of preserving Rangers victories with bogus calls. Next, they recount that a player was ejected from a game in 1996 for crossing himself upon entering the pitch—a deliberately provocative gesture, the referee called it.

In the mainstream press, there is a phrase to describe these complaints: Celtic paranoia. The notion is that Catholics have imagined the crimes committed against them, have grown too attached to the idea of suffering. This smells of victim blaming, but the closer one examines the evidence the more reasonable the thesis becomes. Celtic fans have a predilection for dredging up ancient history and conflating it with recent events. Burns's Jesuitical study, for example, relies on newspaper clippings from the 1960s to make the case against the Scottish referees.

In a way, this confusion of past and present perfectly captures the Scottish Catholic condition. Without question, they continue to suffer prejudice in the present day. But when asked to give examples of the wounds inflicted by Scottish Protestants, they fall back on stories they've inherited from their fathers and grandfathers. To be sure, these are often devastating tales: Catholics denied jobs, shut out of universities, and prevented from falling in love with Protestant women. Western Scotland had been a place, in the words of the novelist Andrew O'Hagan, where "the birds on the trees sang sectarian songs."

But the memories of the past are so easily accessible that they shade perceptions of the present. When commentators call for creation of a new secular school system that would abolish funding for parochial institutions, some Catholics smell the second coming of John Knox. "We must try to be invisible or suffer the inevitable discriminatory consequences," the literary critic Patrick Reilly has fumed in response. They complained vociferously when the newly created Scottish parliament took up residence in the old Assembly Hall of the Church of Scotland. Never mind that the Church of Scotland, like the rest of mainline Protestantism, has become a bastion of bleeding-heart liberalism, racked with guilt over its anti-Catholic past. And never mind that parliament only occupied the building for temporary accommodation.

While discrimination might not exist in spades, prejudice does. Sitting in Ibrox, listening to the taunts of Rangers supporters, Catholics know for certain that some of these fanatics are members of the Scottish parliament and critics of Catholic schools. It's hard not to be wary.

IV.

With Dummy's Guinness-stained gray sweatshirt and blue jeans, he looks undeniably like a soccer fan. Donald Findlay does not. He wears a three-piece suit with striped pants and a navy jacket constructed from lush Saville Row cloth. Across his vest, a gold pocket watch chain holds a miniature crown and family keepsakes. His Gilbert-and-Sullivan facial hair covers his cheeks and then stops at his chin. At Ibrox, they affectionately refer to him as Muttonchops. In his career as one of Scotland's greatest barristers, he evinced a melodramatic persona to match his overwrought attire. Findlay achieved his infamy by freeing some of his hardest clients, including hooligans on both sides of the Old Firm. His flowery oratory flooded the jury box with tears.

After the match, I met Findlay at a hotel bar. Despite a legal career filled with high-profile successes, he will always be best known for his time as the flamboyant vice-chairman of Rangers. Attending games at Celtic Park, he'd sit in the box reserved for the opposing management. He'd deliberately show disdain for his surroundings, kicking up his wingtips and placing them on the box's polished wood. Besieged by a torrent of verbal abuses from Celtic fans, he'd take long drags on his pipe, appearing utterly unmoved. When his Rangers scored goals, Findlay liked to celebrate as ostentatiously and gleefully as possible, the only man standing and cheering amid a sea of dejection. In interviews, he'd go a step further. He made a running gag out of the fact that he didn't celebrate his birthday, because it fell on St. Patrick's Day. Instead, he said that he celebrated on July twelfth, the anniversary of King Billy's triumph. In his living room, he would stage Orange marches.

On a May night in 1999, his tenure at Rangers
came to an abrupt end. Findlay sang, "We're up to our
knees in Fenian Blood" on the karaoke machine, his
arm drunkenly draped over a player's shoulder. He had
gathered with the rest of the Rangers club to celebrate a
victory over Celtic. In his jubilation, he had repeated
lyrics that Rangers supporters blare on a weekly basis,
that leading lights of society had sung for generations.
Most of them, however, hadn't been captured on a video
that would be handed over to the *Daily Record*. On the
same spring evening that Findlay raised his pint glass
and damned the papists, Rangers' darkest impulses
were responsible for dark acts. Rangers fans stabbed,
shot, and beat senseless three young Celtic supporters.
They murdered one and left another in critical condition.

If these events hadn't coincided, perhaps Findlay
could have defended himself in the press. But the environment wouldn't stand for any excuses. The morning that the Findlay story broke in the paper, he
resigned from Rangers management. Over the next few
months, as Scottish eminences lined up to condemn
him, he purchased pills and flirted with suicide. St.
Andrews University, where he had just finished a six-
year term as rector, canceled its plans to award Findlay
an honorary degree. The Scottish Faculty of Advocates,
the body governing the nation's lawyers, fined him
3,500 pounds.

Findlay had become the touchstone for a nation-
wide debate. Delivering the keynote at the Edinburgh
Festival, Scotland's great composer James MacMillan
declared, "Donald Findlay is not a one-off. To believe
that is self-delusion because our [society is] jam-packed

with people like Donald Findlay." He argued that Scotland suffered from a case of "sleepwalking bigotry." Newspaper columnists pronounced Findlay a national stain. But he had his defenders, too. Even some of the management at Celtic testified to Findlay's good heart. In effect, the Donald Findlay debate cut to an essential question of the Old Firm: When they talked about murder and terrorism, was it just good fun or an expression of rotten consciences?

Nearly three years after the videotape, Findlay remains one of the five wealthiest barristers in Scotland. He has rehabilitated himself just enough to become a fairly regular newspaper and television pundit. The Tory party in Scotland doesn't really have a more prominent spokesman. Yet, he can't put the episode behind him. It haunts and obsesses him. When Findlay agreed to meet me, I devised clever plans to coax him onto the subject of the tape. He immediately renders them superfluous. "About the tapes: I should have put up a fight. I would try to challenge them to provide one human being who'd been adversely affected by me because of religion, color, or anything else." Fighting the politically correct elites, he would have proven that the songs are essentially harmless traditions: "It's about getting into the opposition's head; it's a game; it's in the context of football. Do you want to be up to your knees in Fenian blood? Don't be ridiculous."

Like many of the staunchest supporters of Rangers, he didn't grow up in Glasgow. He came from the east of Scotland, a small town called Cowdenbeath, born into a staunchly Tory working-class family. And like most Rangers supporters, he doesn't believe in the Protestantism that his team represents. "I've got no religious beliefs. Believe me, I've tried hard but you can't teach that." What he did inherit was a belief in the monarchy and the British union that disparaged the Scottish-Catholic affection for the Irish motherland. He jokingly, I think, announces his preferred test for British citizenship: If a troop carrying Queen's colors "doesn't bring tears to your eyes, then fuck off!"

It's easy to link support for a soccer club with religiosity. But in an important way, Rangers has actually replaced the Church of Scotland. It allows men like Findlay to join the tradition and institutions of their forefathers, to allay fears about abandoning history without having to embrace their forefathers' eschatology.

Findlay splays across our booth, his pants pulling up past his ankle. He enjoys his cigarillos. From the moment we meet, he advertises himself as a provocateur. By the middle of our conversation, he provokes. "The one absolute barrier is that you must never prejudice a man for his religion. If I wanted to hire a black, lesbian, Catholic, great. But are you not entitled to say that you have no time for the Catholic religion, that it involves the worships of idols?" The statement is structured rhetorically, like a law school professor's hypothetical. With his academic tone, I expect the defamations of the Catholic faith to stop after he has made his point. They don't. "Why can't you be forgiven for thinking that confessing to a priest who is confessing to God is ridiculous and offensive? Or that the pope is a man of perdition?" A bit later he suggests that Scots should have the right to say "that priests immerse themselves in jewels and wealth while they live amid poverty."

Scottish society is a paradox. It has more or less eradicated discrimination in the public sphere. Catholics have their fair share of representation in the universities and workforce. Nevertheless, bigotry against them persists. There was no civil rights movement to sweep away anti-Catholicism—discrimination only faded thanks to globalization. Glasgow's shipyards and steel mills, which had practiced blatantly anti-Catholic hiring, folded in the wake of the '73 oil shocks. Much of the industry that survived came under the ownership of Americans and Japanese, a new economic order that came from "places where they are not nearly so obsessed with defending Derry's walls against the Whore of Babylon," as the critic Patrick Reilly has put it. Catholics gained their social equality without forcing Scotland into a reckoning with its deeply held beliefs. That's why Scottish society continues to harbor, and even reward, Donald Findlay, Rangers fans, and their ideology.

V.

A day after the Old Firm match, I travel to Belfast on the choppy winter sea. The last major Irish migration to Scotland ended about forty years ago. Each time Celtic and Rangers play, however, there's a demographic ripple. Several thousand Northern Irish, Catholics and Protestants, ride the ferry to Glasgow to see the Old Firm. Several thousand make the trip. A sociologist

called Raymond Boyle has determined that eighty percent of Celtic fans in Belfast make sixteen voyages a year
to see their club. To finance these ventures, they must
spend hundreds, sometimes thousands, of pounds.

By the time I catch the boat, the vast bulk of the
supporters has already gone home. Only the hardcore,
who want to squeeze every last pint of lager out of their
weekend, remain. A contingent from Carrickfergus, 10
minutes up the coast from Belfast, had started on Friday, after a half-day on their jobs as lorry drivers, construction workers, and barmaids. Some didn't even
have tickets to the game and little hope of scoring one.
They began drinking upon boarding the ferry, which
has two bars serving a definitive selection of alcohol,
and never really stopped. Jimmy, the thirty-two-year-old
unofficial leader of the group, slept in Glasgow on a
friend's floor with a bottle of wine by his side to stave
off uncomfortable vicissitudes in his blood-alcohol
level. On the ship back to Belfast, with his wife awaiting
his arrival, Jimmy has another five pints.

Because the ferry often carries both Celtic and
Rangers fans, there's usually an unspoken code of
behavior. Supporters of the home crowd can sing as
loudly and obnoxiously as they please. Meanwhile, the
small groups supporting the visiting team don't acknowledge their affiliation or object to their opponents. Since
this is the last Sunday night ferry, the crossing contains
plenty of Rangers fans, this week's home team, but it also
contains couples who've spent the weekend shopping
in Glasgow and middle-class folk who visited relatives.
Only the loud, sloppy drunks in the back of the boat
clearly indicate that an Old Firm match has taken place.

Most of the Rangers fans on this late boat adhere to a new set of etiquette. In this highly mixed crowd, inevitably packed with Catholics, taunting is verboten. The drunkenness of the Carrickfergus crew, however, prevents the practice of restraint. Jimmy, scrawny, blond, and dressed in a track suit, leads the group through a song list in the spirit of unabashed triumphalism. They don't really converse; just go from song to song. At the mere mention of a phrase—"top of the league," "King Billy," "shit Fenian bastard"—they're off.

Because I buy a round of drinks, they enthusiastically welcome me. Jimmy asks me to pile into an already crammed corner of the ship. "Whatever you want to know, I've got it. Ask away. I'll answer anything."

But before I can ask him anything, he begins to boast about his friendship with the guy who dresses as the Rangers team mascot. In the background, Jimmy's traveling companions sing their anti-Catholic medley, repeating the phrase "Fuck the pope" with particular relish.

Jimmy joins them, and then puts his beer on the table and his arm on my shoulder. "Say, 'Fuck the pope,' Frankie boy," he implores me. "We won't talk to you until you say it. Come on, 'Fuck the pope.' It feels good to say it."

Jimmy's minions—two twenty-something women, an older mustachioed carpenter named John Boy, Ralphie the lorry driver, and about six younger guys—take their leader's cue. They begin clapping and chanting rhythmically, "Fuck the pope!" One of the women is most strident: "Don't be a fuckin' Fenian, Frankie. 'Fuck the pope,' come on." I shrug my shoulders, look around the ship to see if anyone else is watching, and try to recite the phrase as a rhetorical question. To the tune of "Camptown Races," they begin to sing, as if planned in advance, "Frankie's a sectarian. Doo-dahh, doo-dahh."

It's obvious that the repeated and vociferous use of the phrase "Fuck the pope" hardly endears us to the rest of the boat. For the entire trip, Jimmy has traded looks with a middle-aged man in a sweater. Another group in a nearby bank of seats has been muttering about the songs. "Ruining our trip, they are. I didn't pay forty quid to be insulted like this," a woman complains to a stewardess. A few moments later, the stewardess approaches us. She leans over and says, "I'm sorry. You've got to stop. It's the rules. It's in your interest to stop." Apparently, this is the third time that she has reproached the group. When we arrive in Belfast, she says, security will be waiting to deal with us. Under normal, more sober circumstances, the threat might have meant something. "Okay. Fine," Jimmy tells her and then points his finger at me, "It was this American sectarian causing all the trouble." Once again, he starts singing my name. The stewardess rises and walks away.

The connection between Scotland and Ireland—or more precisely, the connection between Glasgow and Belfast—runs deep. You can see it across Belfast. In downtown, both Celtic and Rangers have shops selling their gear. Around the city, the Rangers fan clubs double as the lodges for the Orange Order. A cab driver called Billy takes me to his club in the middle of a neighborhood that had once been Protestant, but had almost overnight turned Catholic. His club has a bar, a billiards table, a TV set for watching games, and chairs for meetings. It's a place you can unself-consciously roll up your sleeves and display the "'Gers" tattoo on your forearm. Billy's club stands as the last foothold against inevitable Catholic encroachment in this part of town, a battle-scarred fortress without windows. A tall fence surrounds the building. A Scottish standard flaps atop a pole. Garbage lies scattered through the parking lot in front. "We're more interested in staying than making it look pretty," he apologizes. Across the street, he points to the rubble of a Protestant church. It had been burned to the ground three times.

Old Firm matches, it seems, stir up as much mayhem in Northern Ireland as in Glasgow, if not more. Where the violence in Glasgow takes a desultory pattern, dependent mostly on drunken thugs randomly crossing paths, it occurs regularly in Northern Ireland on the frontiers that separate Catholic and Protestant neighborhoods. The day I arrive from Scotland, a battle had waged through the night, across the province, in the town of Derry. The Old Firm had coincided with an annual Protestant march through town, and the confluence of the two events was explosive. News reports showed the town lit by burning cars, bands of Catholics marching en masse toward the city center to disrupt the Protestant celebrations, police holding their line as the Catholics shot fireworks at them. Stabbings and gunfights were reported.

There's a basic reason for the Northern Irish to embrace the Old Firm with such fervor. They have nothing comparable on their side of the Irish Sea. The country simply can't accommodate it. It wasn't always so. Once upon a time, the city housed a team called Belfast Celtic, ripped off from the original Scottish concept; and it even had its own Protestant rival, a team called Linfield. But in 1949, the Catholic squad folded. Belfast Celtic's management felt that the club could no longer depend on the Protestant police to protect its players and fans. A year earlier, they had watched police cheer Linfield goals. When Linfield's fans invaded the field and began beating players, even breaking legs, the cops stood on the sides. Eventually, all the Catholic clubs in Northern Ireland followed Belfast Celtic in withdrawing from interfaith competition. Stripped of its own rivalries, it was natural that Northern Ireland turned to Scotland.

On the ferry, Jimmy keeps slipping from playfulness into earnest discourse. Sipping his lager, he leans back in a banquette, his sneakers propped up on a table. "Glasgow's not like here." He pauses. "You can walk down the street there in a Rangers top and nothing will happen to you. It's life or death here, mate. They're fucking animals. They'd kill little children." Glasgow, he explains, allows for a strange kind of political escapism. It's not that you leave your politics behind at home. In fact, the opposite occurs. People like Jimmy can indulge their deepest political passions in Scotland. They can indulge them in the most fanatical ways. The difference is that in the safety of the Glasgow soccer stadium they don't have to incessantly calculate the consequences of screaming their beliefs.

Before the ferry lands in Belfast, Jimmy's friends begin to settle themselves into a less frenzied state. One of them had been jumping up and down on the

deck of the ship singing a song called "Bouncy, Bouncy,"
an orange Rangers jersey clinging to his beefy frame. *If
you canny do the Bouncy Bouncy, you're a Tim.* Set
against the night, the fluorescent shirt made him the
only visible sight on the horizon. Disembarking at the
port, he puts on a navy windbreaker and zips it up to
his neck. He looks down at his waist to make sure that
his shirt doesn't hang out from the bottom. Pulling his
blue Nike cap over his eye, he turns back to me. "All
right," he says and fades into the crowd of arrivals.

On the ground in Belfast, passengers keep com-
plaining to cruise officials about our group's behavior.
But the promised security entourage never arrives to
deal with us. In the scheme of Old Firm offenses, these
infractions are too minor to bother with. Waiting for a
conveyor belt to spit out checked luggage, Jimmy sits in
a corner arguing with his wife on the cell phone. He
wants me to cancel my hotel reservation and crash on
his couch. His wife wants to nag him for staying away
all weekend. Before we go to his home, he insists that
we stop for a drink with Ralphie the lorry driver at the
Carrickfergus Glasgow Rangers Club. In Belfast, asking
a cabbie to take you to a Rangers club can be a tricky
business. For that trip, you wouldn't want to gamble
with a Celtic supporter or IRA sympathizer behind the
wheel, especially if you're drunk and intent on flexing
your beer muscles. Jimmy repeatedly tells the driver
that we're headed to the Glasgow Rangers Club and
carefully evaluates each reaction. When the driver's
blank stare remains blank, Jimmy starts singing and
throws his duffle bag into the big black cab.

Settling down, Jimmy calls a girl from Edinburgh

that Ralphie had met at a bar after the game. Ralphie, small, mustachioed, barely comprehensible with his thick Ulster accent, the platonic ideal of a sidekick, has a crush on her. Jimmy hands him the phone, and Ralphie stammers. We laugh at his clumsy flirting. "She's up for it," Jimmy whispers to him. But as the driver turns out from the ferry station and down a dark street, Ralphie abruptly tells the girl that he'll call her later. A look of panic overtakes his face. "Shit man, Jimmy. Fuckin' Falls Road." The Falls Road is a notorious center of IRA activity, a place where a Rangers supporter would be instantaneously mauled. Jimmy grabs the cell phone out of Ralphie's hand and begins to dial friends at the Carrickfergus Rangers Club. They would be our reinforcements— at least they would know where to gather our bruised bodies. "Just tell them you're an American. Nobody would touch you," he counsels. By the time he has dialed the number, a sign for the motorway emerges. Three days of debauchery has deprived them of any sense of geography. Jimmy bangs on the Plexiglas separating the driver from us and gives him the thumbs up. Jimmy and Ralphie break into song, "We're the top of the league, we're the top of the league and you know." As he sings, Jimmy lifts his arms above his head in triumph.

3

How Soccer Explains
the Jewish Question

"Do you want something to read?"
"Yes, do you have something really light?"
"How about this short leaflet: Famous Jewish
Sports Legends."

—*The movie* Airplane!, *1980*

I.

I had grown up thinking that great Jewish athletes
come around about once in a decade, if the gene pool
gets lucky. There was the Los Angeles Dodgers pitcher
Sandy Koufax in the sixties; the swimmer Mark Spitz in
the seventies; and then many fallow years. At home, my
father and I would imagine that various athletes were
quietly Jewish, like the Marrano survivors of the Spanish Inquisition. My father was especially adamant that
Sid Bream, a lanky, energetic first baseman with the
Atlanta Braves, was a person of the book. And, to be
fair, the name, both first and last, made him a plausible

member. But in retrospect, there were biographical
details that probably should have negated our analysis.
Sid Bream liked to talk about his love of hunting, and
he drove a pickup truck. Yes, he wore a Mark Spitz
moustache, but that was twenty years after its vogue
within our community. The simple truth was that we
were too apprehensive to go looking for Bream's real
ethnicity.

Before Bream captured the imagination of our
household, I had stumbled across the soccer club
Hakoah of Vienna, winners of the 1925 Austrian championship. Hakoah's great triumph came at a time when
Austrian soccer represented the world's gold standard
of style and strategy. Although they had only a few
scarce encounters with the other great teams of the era,
Hakoah usually triumphed in these matches. Based on
all the evidence we have, the Jewish all stars were, for a
short spell, one of the best teams on the planet.

Hakoah first came to my attention in a book that I
found rummaging through my uncle's old bedroom, in
my grandparents' house: *Great Jewish Sports Legends.* It
had a frayed blue spine that could be lifted to reveal the
naked binding. Sepia photos filled its pages. When this
volume came into my possession at age eight, it quickly
became a personal favorite. Because it had been written
in the early 1950s, it wasn't so far removed from the
mid-century American renaissance of Jewish athletes,
which consisted of giant figures such as the Chicago
Bears' quarterback Sid Luckman and the Detroit Tigers'
first baseman Hank Greenberg. Like so much of Jewish
life at that moment, the book was schizophrenic about
its ethnic identity. As I remember the book, it was both

a paean to Jewish achievement and to assimilation, but mostly to assimilation. There was no Star of David on the title page and no anecdotes about Greenberg skipping a crucial season-end game to attend Yom Kippur services. That's why Hakoah sprung at me from the pages. There was nothing self-effacing about the Jewishness of the Hakoah players. The team had a Hebrew name and advertised its Judaism on its jersey.

From the start, in other words, Hakoah had seemed chimerical to me. My search for the team made it even more so. I traveled to Vienna with promises of help from academics and community leaders. From them, I began to compile the names of Viennese Jews in their eighties and nineties who might have some memory of the championship season. Since 1940, Viennese Jewry has dwindled from approximately 200,000 to 7,000. Some of these remaining few include immigrants from the old Soviet bloc and a smattering of Israelis who have moved to town for business. The bulk consists of aging natives. Many of them have children in the U.S. and even spent years abroad themselves. But they've come back to the city of their youth for their last days so they can live a familiar lifestyle. Because so many Austrians enthusiastically welcomed the Nazis, they often apologize for continuing to reside in Vienna. A retired professor of economics told me in a perfect American accent, "What can I do? I know the Austrians are the worst. Maybe they would do it all over again. But I have interests here and friends. It's comfortable."

These elderly Jews wanted badly to talk about the past, about politics and their love of the United States, to buy me a meal at a Chinese restaurant and a pastry at a coffee house. Unfortunately, for my purposes, these conversations didn't have anything remotely to do with soccer. None of them had played the game. Their parents considered it too scruffy, violent, and proletarian for their children. Viennese Jews were among the most bourgeois of the bourgeoisie. And even these old Jews were too young to remember Hakoah's glory years during the twenties. "Maybe there's someone in New York you could talk to," they told me. I had gone all the way around the world only to be told that the answers to my queries might be found in the smoked-fish line at Zabar's on Broadway. Sadly, in New York and Florida, where I had more names to contact, I didn't make much more headway. I couldn't. Anyone who might remember Hakoah at its best is too superannuated to remember, or no longer around. As far as I can tell, the historical memory of the club now resides with a gentile Swedish sportswriter from the town of Hässelby called Gunnar Persson who has obsessively tracked every shred of evidence vaguely related to the club. With his help, I began to cobble together the story of the wonder Jews.

Although it seems so strange now, the idea of a professional Jewish soccer club, it is only strange because so few of the Jewish soccer clubs survived Hitler. But, in the 1920s, Jewish soccer clubs had sprouted throughout metropolitan Europe, in Budapest, Berlin, Prague, Innsbruck, and Linz.

Jewish teams cloaked themselves in Jewish, not Hungarian or Austrian or German, nationalism, literally wearing their Zionism on their sleeves and shirts. Decades before Adolf Eichmann forced them to don the yellow star, some of these clubs played with King David's logo stitched onto the breasts of their jerseys. They swathed themselves in blue-and-white uniforms, the colors of Israel. Their unabashedly Hebrew names, Hagibor ("The Hero"), Bar Kochba (after the leader of a second-century revolt against the Romans), and Hakoah ("The Strength"), had unmistakably nationalist overtones.

If all this seemed exceptionally political, it was because these clubs were the products of a political doctrine. An entire movement of Jews believed that soccer, and sport more generally, would liberate them from the violence and tyranny of anti-Semitism. The polemicist Max Nordau, one of the founding fathers of turn-of-the-century Zionism, created a doctrine called *Muskeljudentum*, or muscular Judaism. Nordau argued that the victims of anti-Semitism suffered from their own disease, a condition he called *Judendot*, or Jewish distress. Life in the dirty ghetto had afflicted the Jews with effeminacy and nervousness. "In the narrow Jewish streets," he wrote, "our poor limbs forgot how to move joyfully; in the gloom of sunless houses our eyes became accustomed to nervous blinking; out of fear of constant persecution the timbre of our voices was extinguished to an anxious whisper." To beat back anti-Semitism and eradicate *Judendot*, Jews didn't merely need to reinvent their body politic. They needed to reinvent their bodies. He prescribed *Muskeljudentum* as a cure for this malady. He wrote, "We want to restore to the flabby Jewish body its lost tone, to make it vigorous and strong, nimble and powerful." Jews, he urged in articles and lectures, should invest in creating gymnasia and athletic fields, because sport "will straighten us in body and character."

Muscular Judaism wasn't an egghead's pipe dream. Nordau's high-toned words trickled down to the leaders of Central Europe's Jewish communities. Of the fifty-two Olympic medals captured by Austria between 1896 and 1936, eighteen had been won by Jews—eleven times more than they would have won if they had performed proportional to their population. And while much of the achievement came in individual events, especially fencing and swimming, Jews thrived in soccer, too. During the 1910s and 1920s, a healthy portion of the Hungarian national soccer team consisted of Jews. For a brief moment, Jewish sporting success mimicked Jewish intellectual achievement.

There is something creepy about Max Nordau's description of the sickly, effeminate Jewish body. And the creepiness lies in its similarities to the anti-Semitic caricature. Perhaps it's not a coincidence. Zionism and modern European anti-Semitism dripped out of the same fin-de-siècle intellectual spout. Both movements were born at the turn of the last century, in the midst of another wave of massive globalization and discombobulating social change, when the European intelligentsia reacted strongly against the values of the enlightenment. They embraced a scientific concept of race, an almost homoerotic obsession with perfecting the body, and a romantic idea of the motherland. Neither placed any emphasis on the universal brotherhood of man, the ideal of the French Revolution.

But that counter-enlightenment phase passed long ago, defeated in war and intellectually discredited. The last fifty years of European politics has run hard in the opposite direction, a return to the celebration of reason and universalism. Certainly, that's the theory behind the European Union, which assumes that conflicts can be avoided with dialogue and that commonality of interest can transcend even the deepest enmity.

This liberalization of thinking hasn't purged anti-Semitism from the European system. By most counts, continental anti-Semitism is as pervasive as it has ever been in the postwar era, or even more so. It certainly exists within European soccer. But that doesn't mean that European anti-Semitism is the same now as before the war. It's an entirely different beast, one not nearly as likely to kill, that has been made less pernicious by globalization's transformation of Europe. Thanks to the immigration of Africans and Asians, Jews have been replaced as the primary objects of European hate. These changes can be seen in microcosm in the history of Jewish soccer. But before explaining the present, it is necessary to go back and tell the story of Vienna's Hakoah.

II.

At the beginning of the last century, revolutionary movements, of the left and the right, understood the political mileage to be gained from soccer. Socialist youth clubs sponsored teams, and aspiring fascists tried to hitch themselves to popular clubs. In Vienna, a small circle of Zionist intellectuals saw the same potential in the game. This group included a dentist, a lawyer, and Fritz Beda-Löhrner, the cabaret librettist who wrote "Yes, We Have No Bananas." They, too, wanted the game to propagandize on behalf of their movement.

In 1909, this group created the Hakoah athletic club in the spirit of Max Nordau. Its name translates from Hebrew as strength, and that was the Nordauesque point of the club: to project strength. The team was meant to burst stereotypes, but in one important respect it confirmed them. Before any other club in the world, Hakoah thoroughly embraced the marketplace. It paid its players and paid them well—about three times the salary of the average worker. These higher wages, along with the ideological mission, helped Hakoah assemble an all-star team of Jewish players recruited from across Austria and Hungary. While the club only fielded Jewish players, it brought in the best gentiles to coach them, including Englishmen who instilled the latest in strategy.

There was a danger inherent in the Hakoah concept. Viennese anti-Semites generally didn't need a pretext to shout bile or pick fights, but Hakoah gave them a perfect one. Common shouts from opposing fans included *Drecskjude* (dirty Jew) and the oxymoronic *Judensau* (Jewish pig). To give their fans some confidence that they could escape this environment alive, Hakoah plucked a corps of bodyguards from the wrestling and boxing clubs that it also ran. The most iconic Jewish self-defender was the wrestler Mickey Herschel. In photos, he looks like a Charles Atlas character, in a bikini brief with a musculature that seems

impossible in a world before protein shakes and ana-
bolic steroids. Herschel and his corps evolved into a
community security force that sometimes stood outside
synagogues and neighborhoods, casting appropriately
goonish glances at prospective pogrom participants.

From the newspaper accounts of the period, it's not
at all clear that the Jewish team possessed superior talent. But the clippings do make mention of the enthusiastic Jewish supporters and the grit of the players. The
grittiest performance of them all came at the greatest
moment in Hakoah history. In the third to last game of
the 1924–25 season, an opposing player barreled into
Hakoah's Hungarian-born goalkeeper Alexander Fabian
as he handled the ball. Fabian toppled onto his arm,
injuring it so badly that he could no longer plausibly
continue in goal. This was not an easily remediable
problem. The rules of the day precluded substitutions
in any circumstance. So Fabian returned to the game
with his arm in a sling and swapped positions with a
teammate, moving up into attack on the outside right.
Seven minutes after the calamitous injury, Hakoah
blitzed forward on a counterattack. A player called Erno
Schwarz landed the ball at Fabian's feet. With nine
minutes remaining in the game, Fabian scored the goal
that won the game and clinched Hakoah's championship.

In a way, Hakoah achieved just what its founders
had hoped for: A victorious team trailed by a bandwagon of Jews. The same Jewish elites who dismissed
the game as the province of working-class ruffians
began to bankroll Hakoah, believing that the respect of
gentiles it acquired might rub off on them. Assimilated

Jews who didn't like to acknowledge or flaunt their
identity in front of gentiles began filling Hakoah's
18,000-seat stadium in Vienna's second district. They
told each other tales of how a gentile—who wanted
Hakoah to beat a rival of his own club—shouted "Go Mr.
Jew," a massively respectful cheer relative to the rest. As
Edmund Schechter, an American diplomat, recounted
in a memoir of his Viennese youth, "Each Hakoah victory become another proof that the period of Jewish
inferiority in physical activities had come to an end."

Just as they built their squad using the methods of
modern management, Hakoah exploited their successes
with a marketing plan that could have been scripted by a
Wharton MBA. In the off season, Hakoah toured the
world, the same way that Manchester United now builds
its brand with jaunts to the Far East and America. Instead
of selling jerseys, however, Hakoah sold Zionism. Preparing for visits, Hakoah would send ahead promoters to
generate buzz for *Muskeljudentum* and distribute tickets to
companies stocked with Jewish employees. They lured
overwhelming crowds to watch this curiosity. In New
York, Hakoah pulled 46,000 fans into the Polo Grounds.
Lithuanian Jews bicycled through the night to see the
club. Such audiences lifted Hakoah's game to levels far
above its natural talent. Against the London outfit West
Ham United, the Jews ran up a 5–1 victory. Naysayers
rightly point to the West Ham lineup on that day. And it's
true, the Hammers didn't take the traveling Jews very seriously, playing a mostly reserve squad. Nevertheless, the
achievement stands: Before Hakoah, no continental team
had beaten an English club on English soil, the same soil
on which the game had been created.

There was, however, an unintended consequence of this success. On the team's 1925 trip, Hakoah players caught a glimpse of New York City, a metropolis seemingly uninfected by European anti-Semitism. It replaced Jerusalem as their Zion, and, over the next year, they immigrated there en masse. Deprived of nine of its best players, Hakoah attempted resurrection but only achieved mediocrity. For the rest of its brief life, it struggled to hold down a place in the top division of Austrian football, occasionally plummeting out of it. And then, its players struggled against death. With the 1938 *Anschluss* and German rule of the nation, the Austrian league shut down Hakoah, nullified the results of any games played against Hakoah, and it handed over the club's stadium to the Nazis.

When I returned to Washington from Vienna, I went to the library of the national Holocaust Museum. A scholar had pointed me in the direction of a documentary that contained footage of Hakoah players. *Der Führer Schenkt den Juden Eine Stadt, The Fuhrer Gives a City to the Jews,* depicts life in the Czech concentration camp of Theresienstadt. The Nazis had created Theresienstadt as a Potemkin village that they would show to the Red Cross, Danes, and other humanitarians. Here, the Jews attended lectures and performed symphonies. How could there be genocide?

So pleased with their ability to pull the wool over the humanitarian eyes, the Nazis intended to stage Theresienstadt for a far wider audience. They would transpose the images to celluloid and distribute them widely. In the summer of 1944, the Nazis commissioned the burly Jewish comic actor and director Kurt Gerron to make the picture. Gerron had become a big name in the Weimar film renaissance, a colleague of Marlene Dietrich. But now, he wasn't just shooting for his reputation; he believed that he could make a film that could please the SS enough to save his life.

The Nazis had given Gerron an impossible task. They had asked him to make a film without giving him any control over the script or editing. In fact, he died in Auschwitz without having viewed any of the 17,000 feet of film that he shot. More than that, the residents of Theresienstadt didn't lend themselves to propaganda. Not even modern special effects could have compensated for the sad faces playing chess or the grim urgency with which children grab pieces of buttered bread off a plate.

To please the Nazis, Gerron embraced the Nazi style—especially their cult of the body. Women perform aerobics in short shorts. A shirtless worker brings down his hammer on an anvil holding piping steel. A group of men play soccer. It is the perverse Nazi inversion of *Muskeljudentum*.

NARRATOR: Use of free time is left to individuals. Often workers flock to soccer games, Theresienstadt's major sports event.
The courtyard of the camp's old military barracks is used as a field. Men and little boys cram the porticos overlooking the dirt pitch. The camera pans to teams dashing into barracks. Like Hakoah, one team wears Jewish stars on its white jerseys. The other wears dark shirts.

NARRATOR: The teams each have only seven men, due to limited space.

Players shake hands with the referee.

NARRATOR: Nevertheless, enthusiastic fans watch a spirited game from beginning to end.

Play begins. Some of the players in dark jerseys must have played professionally. Despite the cramped quarters, they execute sly give-and-gos and skillfully deflect a corner kick into the goal. With each goal, the crowd jumps ecstatically from their seats.

For two minutes, the action unfolds without narration. The scene then abruptly switches to the bathing facilities, a tribute to the compound's impeccable hygiene. A line of naked men marches into the showers.

III.

It's not exactly breaking news that, sixty years after Hakoah, anti-Semitism persists in Europe. There are even signs—the flourishing of ultra-right politicians in France and Austria; a rise in physical violence directed at French Jewry; political cartoons redolent of classic hook-nose stereotypes—that it may be increasing. As scary as all that is, intellectual honesty demands a distinction between anti-Semitism then and now.

Anti-Semitism now is something strange and new—not quite socially acceptable and not quite unacceptable, either. There's perhaps no stranger case of this attitude toward the Jews than Tottenham, a soccer team based in North London. Tottenham's fans refer to themselves as the Yids or the Yiddoes. When the name comes off their lips in a Cockney accent, it sounds like a crude slur. And, it's true, the name doesn't have the nicest connotations. When the English fascist Oswald Mosley's gangs marched through the Jewish East End of London in 1936, they shouted, "Down with the Yids." Throughout history, plenty of other Jew haters have used the term in exactly this fashion. But Tottenham fans actually apply the moniker to themselves in a complimentary, prideful way.

When a Tottenham player threads a pass or slams a shot from outside the penalty area, the fans celebrate him by chanting, "Yiddo, Yiddo." To rally their club at moments of unsure play, Tottenham fans stir their beloved club with the song "Who, who, who let the Yiddos out?" They serenade their favorite players as "Jews," even though none of them qualify under the loosest standards of *halakhah*. When the great blond German striker Jürgen Klinsmann arrived at the club in 1994, fans honored him by singing:

> *Chim-chiminee, chim-chiminee*
> *Chim-chim churoo*
> *Jürgen was a German*
> *But now he's a Jew.*

To the uninitiated, the logic undergirding the connection between Tottenham and the Jews isn't obvious. For that matter, the logic probably doesn't seem any clearer to Tottenham's fans—it's just an inherited custom practiced without thought. But as far as I can discern, the historical link is this: While lots of London neighborhoods had Jews, the Stamford Hill neighborhood near the Tottenham grounds had lots of Hasidic Jews, black-clad, pre-modern, and unassimilated, the kind that stick out. They provided a large rack on which Tottenham's enemies could hang their hatreds. The fans that persecuted Tottenham for its neighborhood Jews included almost every club in the league, but the worst were their cross-town rivals from Chelsea. Even though they had nearly as many Jewish supporters as Tottenham, Chelsea composed some exceptionally hateful tunes. One went, "Hitler's gonna gas 'em again/We can't stop them/The Yids from Tottenham." Another urged, "Gas a Jew, Jew, Jew, put him in the oven, cook him through."

How do you respond to such bile? Tottenham's strategy alternated between ignoring the chants and changing the subject with insults of their own. Neither approach made much headway. When they finally devised a response, they borrowed a classical argumentative act of legerdemain, claiming the insult as a badge of honor. The key moment in this transformation came in an away game against Manchester City in the early 1980s. Tottenham's opponents subjected them to a song that went,

> We'll be running around Tottenham with our pricks
>   hanging out tonight,
> We'll be running around Tottenham with our pricks
>   hanging out tonight,
> Singing I've got a foreskin, I've got a foreskin, I've
>   got a foreskin, and you ain't
> We've got foreskins, we've got foreskins, you ain't.

Instead of passively absorbing the blow, Tottenham rounded up its Jewish supporters, encouraged them to drop their pants, and defiantly wave their circumcised members. It was a retort so funny, so impossible to rebut that Tottenham effectively closed down the argument.

Strangely, it was the hooligan element, the same one with members tied to the far right, which adopted the Jewish identity first. They named their band of thugs "The Yid Army," and they made the Israeli flag their standard. After victorious battles against rival gangs, they would rub their triumph in their enemies' faces by dancing around them and chanting, "Yiddo." Hooligans may sound like marginal fans, but they weren't. Up until the nineties, they were regarded by many average fans as a vanguard, fashion-setters who deserved respect for their maniacal devotion to the club. So Tottenham's Jewish identity quickly spread from the hardcore to the average fan, becoming part of the fabric of the culture of the club. Before games, the streets leading to the stadium become a storefront for vendors with T-shirts covered with proclamations like "Yid4ever."

Some of the greatest clubs in European soccer—Bayern Munich, Austria Wien, AS Roma—have been pegged by detractors as "Jewish" clubs. In most cases, it's because their early supporters came from the ranks of the pre–World War I Jewish bourgeoisie. Only one club in the world, however, can out-Jew Tottenham. Ajax of Amsterdam decorate their stadium with Israeli flags, which can be purchased on game day just outside the stadium. The unforgettable site of blond-haired Dutchmen with beer guts and red Stars of David painted on their foreheads accompanies Ajax matches. And unlike Tottenham's official organization, which does nothing to encourage its Jewish identification, Ajax has made Judaism part of its ethos.

During the 1960s, Ajax cut the European game loose from its stodgy strategies, rubbishing traditional rigid defensive formations and embracing a more creative approach that eschewed assigning stringent positions. The press called their style Total Football. The auteur behind this new aesthetic was the great player and philo-Semite Johann Cruyff. His club's strange pregame rituals included the delivery of a kosher salami, and locker-room banter self-consciously peppered with Yiddish phrases. Before every game, a player called Jaap Van Praag would crack a Jewish joke. The club's Jewish physiotherapist has recounted, "The players liked to be Jewish even though they weren't." Israelis were more charmed by these customs than anyone. As Simon Kuper explains in his book *Ajax: The Dutch, the War,* many Israelis believe that Cruyff is himself a Jew. This, of course, is urban legend, but a legend he feeds. When he visits Israel, where his wife's family has relatives, he has been spotted wearing a yarmulke with his number 14 stitched into it.

The daring Cruyff teams were reflective of the hippie youth culture overtaking Amsterdam in the sixties. They also represented a philo-Semitic wave overtaking the city. In those years, more than any country in Europe, the Dutch aided Israel and stood up for the

Jewish state in the United Nations. During the 1973 oil boycott, the Dutch prime minister rode a bike in front of TV cameras to show his solidarity with the Israelis. At the height of this moment, Amsterdam elected a string of Jewish mayors. There was a cultural context for these moves: The Dutch had begun to rediscover and celebrate their history of resisting the Nazi invasion. Starting in the sixties, annual commemorations trumpeted the heroism of a February 1941 mass strike that had been waged to protest the Nazi occupation. And the Dutch did as much as anyone to cultivate the cult of Anne Frank and the righteous gentiles who guarded her family in an Amsterdam attic.

But more than rediscovering this history of resistance, the Dutch fabricated it. As historians have pointed out tirelessly in recent years, the Dutch did a better job collaborating with the Nazis than stopping them. Holland lost a higher percentage of its Jews to the Holocaust than any other country. In cosmopolitan, tolerant Amsterdam, identifying with the Jews in the Ajax style fit this project of reinvention and guilt assuagement. David Winner, an English journalist who wrote *Brilliant Orange: The Neurotic Genius of Dutch Soccer,* argues that Ajax engages in an "unconscious act of post-Holocaust solidarity with the city's murdered, missing Jews."

This is a generous interpretation, and it may contain some significant sociological truth. But it's a bit too sympathetic to the Dutch quest for redemption. The Dutch haven't come as far as they like to believe. Empathy for the Jews in the soccer stadium has dark underpinnings. The essence of anti-Semitism has been the treatment of the Jews as something alien, as dangerous interlopers, a state within the state. For two hundred years, a significant swath of European Jews struggled to move past these canards. Even Zionists like Max Nordau, who touted the idea of the Jewish state, ultimately craved nothing more than acceptance as full-fledged Europeans. They dreamed of assimilation.

Unfortunately, after the Holocaust and the founding of Israel, this acceptance still hasn't really arrived. Even when the Europeans identify with the Jews, as in the Ajax and Tottenham cases, they confirm that the Jews are foreigners, not like themselves. They still treat Jews as bizarre curiosities, reducing them to alien symbols—yarmulkes, sideburns, a Star of David.

There's a parallel to the American use of Indians as their sporting mascots, as in the case of the Washington Redskins, Cleveland Indians, and Florida State Seminoles. It is possible to argue that these nicknames are compliments, a tribute to the bravery and fighting spirit of the Native Americans. And isn't obeisance a better way to treat the aborigines than slaughtering them? But there's a sizeable flaw in this reasoning. Americans can only pay this kind of obeisance because they have slaughtered the Indians. Nobody is around to object to turning them into cartoon images. This perversely worsens the problem. The cartoon images of the mascots freeze the Indians in time, portraying them as they lived in the nineteenth century at the time of the west's conquest, wearing leather suits and feather headdresses. It becomes impossible to imagine the remaining Indians ever transcending their primitivism, ever leaving their reservations and assimilating into society.

The same sort of cartoon image has afflicted the European Jews. No matter how hard they try, they're stuck as outsiders and "others" in the continental mind. This treatment confirms an old aphorism, a bit strong but still truthful: a philo-Semite is an anti-Semite who loves Jews.

But to leave the argument there is a bit too simple. Europe has come a long way since the war. In part, it has changed on its own. It recoiled against the horrific deeds that it had committed—and it has swung into a militant opposition to racialism, militarism, and nationalism. Ironically, this political correctness has made it irrationally uncomfortable with Israel's unapologetic defense of Jewish nationhood and insistence on military response to terrorism. When Europe descends into anti-Semitism, it's now motivated more by an uncompromising commitment to enlightenment ideals than inherited hatred toward Christ killers. Mark Lilla, the University of Chicago political theorist, has written, "Once upon a time, the Jews were mocked for not having a nation-state. Now they are criticized for having one." He continues, "Many Western European intellectuals, including those whose toleration and even affection for Jews cannot be questioned, find [Israel] incomprehensible. The reason is not anti-Semitism nor even anti-Zionism in the usual sense. It is that Israel is, and is proud to be, a nation-state—the nation-state of the Jews. And that is profoundly embarrassing to post-national Europe."

Europe has also changed because of globalization. Most noticeably, the continent has been inundated with immigrants. Before the war, Jews and Gypsies were the outsiders who bore the brunt of European culture's contempt for otherness. The arrival of Senegalese, Pakistanis, and Chinese hasn't endowed European nationalism with a significantly more multi-ethnic idea of the state. But it has diffused hatred, so that it doesn't fix on a single ethnic group worthy of elimination. You can see this in the soccer stadium very clearly. Raw anti-Semitism is anomalous. Most of the hatred in soccer now focuses on blacks in the form of ape noises and racist taunts emanating from the crowd and players. And outside the stadium, it is often Muslims who now suffer bigotry of the majority.

Just as important, the so-called Jewish soccer clubs like Tottenham and Ajax are a major leap forward from pogroms and *Einsatzgruppen*. Instead of denouncing the Jews as pollutants to the nation, chunks of the working class have identified themselves as Jewish, even if only in the spirit of irony.

Of course, there remain places in Europe with far less irony than others.

IV.

Outside the stadium in the old German quarter of southern Budapest, the police line up fans and frisk them. Although they weed out knives and projectiles, they're much more interested in preventing the entry of painted banners that bring unwanted attention to their country. It's testimony to Hungarian policing—or perhaps to the determination of fans—that they rarely achieve their goal. Supporters of the club Ferencvaros wrap the banners around their bodies and conceal them beneath their clothes. Before games, they unfurl the sheets so that they extend over entire rows. One begins, "The trains are leaving. . . ." The second concludes, ". . . for Auschwitz."

This slogan is pretty much all you need to know about the atmosphere in the arena. But what makes Ferencvaros so impressive isn't just the depth of their hatred; it's the breadth of it. They have an unending array of Dr. Mengele–inspired songs and chants. Lyrics typical of the genre include, "Dirty Jews, dirty Jews, gas chambers, gas chambers." Another set repeats the mantra, "Soap, bones." As if the death camp imagery wasn't clear enough, Ferencvaros fans press their tongues into their palates to produce a hissing that mimics the release of Zyklon B. For a time in the nineties, they would punctuate the celebration of goals with an extension of the arm into a Nürnberg-style salute.

Ferencvaros aren't especially careful about whom they tar as "Dirty Jews." Most all their Hungarian opponents get smeared this way. But they reserve their most hateful behavior for one longtime archenemy, another Budapest club called MTK Hungaria. In fairness, Ferencvaros are far from alone in smearing MTK.

At a glance, this disdain looks like resentment. MTK has a long record of success. The team has won twenty-one national championships and finished second eighteen times. With a deep-pocketed owner, they have ushered in a recent renaissance, taking three of the last five Hungarian Cups to the victory stand. Usually, a winning streak like this builds a sturdy bandwagon that runs roughshod over the resenters. Eight-year-old boys can't resist attaching themselves to a juggernaut. Adult fans, who remain closeted when their team muddles along, proudly announce their allegiance by hanging an emblem from their car's rearview mirror. But the strange fact about MTK is that their success has brought no such increase in their following. Even during championship seasons, it's lucky if it can attract more than a thousand of its own supporters to home games. Followers of the visiting team frequently outnumber them.

The management of MTK won't officially admit it, but its supporters will: The reason it has so few fans and so many enemies is because it is a Jewish club. That is to say, MTK was founded by downtown Jewish businessmen in 1888, and in the early twentieth century the team consisted largely of Jewish players. Before the end of World War I, this wasn't such a terrible stigma. Jews had been early and fiery promoters of Hungarian nationalism. Unlike Hakoah, MTK had no Zionist agenda. In fact, the M in MTK stood for Magyar, explicitly tethering the club's Jews to the cause of Hungarian nationalism. The team even self-consciously placed its stadium on the Hungaria Road. In return for their fidelity to the cause, the Jews won acceptance in Budapest society. The city's accommodating atmosphere swelled the community into one of the most massive aggregations of Jews on the planet, so much so that James Joyce, among others, dubbed it "Judapest."

After the breakdown of the Hapsburg Empire and Hungary's disastrous experiment with communist revolution in 1919, this comfortable coexistence ended.

Jews emerged as the nationalist politicians' scapegoat
of choice. These politicians, and their newspapers,
homed in on MTK as a potent symbol of the pernicious-
ness of the Jew. They ascribed the crudest anti-Semitic
stereotypes to the club—money grubbing, rootless
mercenaries, dirty players. In the forties, these nationalists came to power and aligned themselves with the
Nazis. They shuttered MTK entirely because of its ethnic affiliation. After World War II swept out these Iron
Cross fascists, the communists reopened MTK for business. The party handed control of the club to a succession of patrons from the trade unions and secret police.

But no matter the patron, the club's identity has
never changed. Despite the many efforts of supporters
and management, the perception of Jewishness could
never be scrubbed from MTK. Even now, in the democratic era, as Hungary enters the European Union, very
few gentiles support MTK. It still means crossing a
social barrier that even the most liberal, open-minded
Hungarians don't often traverse. To them, wearing an
MTK jersey is akin to wearing a yarmulke. The result is
that one of the two best teams in Hungary has become
a ghetto in the oldest European sense of the word, a dis-
tillation of the European Jewish condition, the bitter-
sweet mingling of the greatest success and lonely misery.

4

How Soccer Explains
the Sentimental Hooligan

I.

To my knowledge, there is only one example of the converse of Tottenham's Yid Army: a Jewish soccer fan who proudly taunts opposing teams with anti-Semitic insults. I know him by his nom de guerre, Alan Garrison.

His surname is an alias that he adopted almost thirty years ago to complicate dealings with the police. Since the age of five, Alan has supported Tottenham's West London rivals, Chelsea. He deserves his own page in the history book, and not just as an oddity. By the mid-nineteen-sixties, he was a commander in one of the first organized crews of English soccer hooligans. He practically invented the genre. Under his leadership—that is until he spent much of the seventies and eighties in prison—Chelsea began to emerge as the most storied band of soccer thugs on the planet, the group with the greatest capacity for hate and destruction.

But before describing this contribution to European civilization, I must qualify my characterization of Alan as a Jew. And I admit that this is not a small qualification. Alan Garrison's German father served as a lieutenant in Hitler's SS. The Allies charged him with war crimes committed in the Russian campaign, although they never prosecuted the case. When British troops in the south of France shot him in the stomach and legs, everything in his life suddenly and strangely inverted. The Allies captured his riddled body and mercifully sent it to heal in an Edinburgh military infirmary. As he lay sprawled in his medical dress and entirely dependent on the goodness of his adversary, he fell madly in love with his Scottish-Jewish nurse, and she with him. In 1946, they had Alan, the first of their three Aryan-Jewish children. It was a match made to inflame. Both the mother's family and community ferociously shunned them. When this shame and stigma became too great to bear, they fled with their baby to a new, less fraught, more anonymous life in London.

From the looks of Alan's adult visage—doughy face, droopy eyes, English teeth, big glasses, feathery gray hair—he would have had a hard time on the playground no matter what his pedigree. His mixed parentage didn't help his case on the asphalt. "Dumb kike," the heartless kids would call out one day, kicking and bullying him. "Fuckin' Nazi Hun," they would yell the next, reenacting their anti-Semitic pogrom as a heroic advance against Hitler's bunker.

Alan's identity became a drag. When his mother wanted him to become a Bar Mitzvah, he flatly refused. He told her, poor lady, that he had given up on the Jewish religion all together. From that day forward, he would practice paganism and worship the goddess Isis, part of a faith his art teacher had explained in a course on ancient civilization. Alan made other resolutions to himself. He would become strong. He would take up boxing and use his combinations against any fool who dared insult him. He would do whatever he could to ingratiate himself with the crowd of tough lads. By befriending them, he would be surrounding himself in a protective bubble that could repel all attackers.

On Alan's fifth birthday, his father, now an accountant, gave him a break from the pummeling. He took him to watch their local club, Chelsea, play in the Stamford Bridge stadium. West London in those days didn't yet have sushi restaurants or latte bars. Chelsea, both the neighborhood and the club, had hardly a hint of the glamour or cosmopolitanism that so define it now. On weekdays, dogs would race on the track that wrapped around the soccer field. In the Shed, like large parts of English soccer stadiums before the 1990s, there was no place to sit, just terraces of concrete. You could cram a seemingly unending amount of humanity into these terraces, and the ticket-takers were never really inclined to cut off the flow. The stadium, so filled with passion and camaraderie, overwhelmed Alan. This, too, he wanted in his life. As he got a bit older, he began going to games on his own and grew chummy with the other kids who haunted the Shed. They loved the football, to be sure, but they also liked to behave badly.

They set a new standard for their naughtiness during a 1963 match against a club from the industrial north called Burnley. A few hundred Burnley fans sat in the North Stand of Stamford Bridge, opposite the Shed. Alan and his friends fumed over this presence of so many outsiders. They decided that they would pay a surprise visit to the North Stand and teach Burnley a lesson about the etiquette of visiting Chelsea. Because Alan wasn't even sixteen—and many of his mates were even younger—their attack was easily repelled by a bunch of thirty-year-old men, whose jobs in mechanic shops and factory floors had bequeathed them imposing biceps. "It was a right kicking," Alan recalled to me many years later. Within minutes after he launched the attack, Alan was sent tumbling down several flights of terraces. The young men needed many pints of lager to make the pain go away.

But even the alcohol couldn't erase the humiliation. From that evening in the pub, Alan and his mates began planning a visit to Burnley the next season. Stealth tactics would guide them. They would melt into the Burnley crowd, and only then mount their attack. It worked masterfully. Nobody can be sure how many men of Burnley were sent to the hospital that day. But enough fell that the newspapers took notice. The English press wrote about a menace it called football hooliganism.

II.

When I first met Alan in a pub, he looked like a man who spends a significant amount of time straddling a Harley Davidson. He wore a black satin Oakland Raiders jacket. His hair was short on the sides and thick on the top, a half-mullet. A Wiccan amulet—an inverted pentacle—dangled from his neck on a piece of string. Upon seeing his middle-aged physique, I thought, if worst comes to worst, at least I'll be able to outrun him.

Alan had arrived for our interview twenty minutes late and greeted me brusquely. "All right," he said, shaking my hand, failing to acknowledge his tardiness. I guided him to a table in the corner.

"Let me get you a drink," I offered.

"A Coke. I don't drink," he replied. "I learned the hard way that it disadvantages you in a fight."

Very quickly in our conversation, he ostentatiously advertised his bona fides. "The police have nicked me twenty-one times.... I'm addicted to violence.... I've tried to stop, but I can't." He showed me battle scars, a bump on his wrist from a shattered bone that healed funny; an arm that folds around in a direction that would defy a healthy network of joints and tendons. But in making this presentation, he began to undermine the image he intended. Alan is a compulsive talker, with endless opinions on an endless number of subjects. My pen struggled to match the pace of his pontifications on the deficiencies of authoritarian governments, the morality of the Anglo-American war against Iraq, the genius of Alexander the Great, and the earnest temperament of Californians.

This profusion only came to a stop when he arrived at the subject of his beloved club, Chelsea. "This is a good place for you to visit," he said, motioning toward the bar, "because of its symbolism." The bar takes its name from the old, notorious Shed that once housed the Chelsea toughs. In fact, the bar stands on that very spot. Only now the Shed can be entered from the lobby of a plush hotel—part of a massive upmarket development on the stadium grounds. Around the corner from the pub, it is possible to order lobster at the King's Brasserie. Inside the Shed, professionals in suits laugh over pints. A plasma TV flashes an advertisement for massages and other treatments at the Chelsea Club and Spa on the other side of the stadium.

More than any club in the world, Chelsea has been transformed by globalization and gentrification. It went from the club most closely identified with hooliganism in the eighties to the club most identified with cosmopolitanism in the nineties. The real estate development of Stamford Bridge was only a piece of this. Gentrification could be seen on the pitch, too. Chelsea hired a string of Italian and Dutch eminences to coach the team and leave their flashy foreign imprints. Under their stewardship, Chelsea earned the distinction of becoming the first club in England to field a squad that contained not a single Englishman. Their new panache exacerbated the trend toward the cosmopolitan, attracting a boatload of foreign investment. The Middle Eastern airline Air Emirates began advertising on its jersey. In 2003, the second richest man in Russia, a Jewish oil magnate called Roman Abramovich, bought a majority stake in the club and began to spend his fortune constructing a championship-caliber team.

To many, Alan included, these improvements felt like a nasty swipe at the club's working-class base, as if the team had dropped its most loyal fans for the ephemeral affiliations of the trend-conscious effete. Of the many changes, there was a single moment that hurt most. In 1983, Chelsea's chairman Ken Bates proposed encasing fans in a 12-volt electrical fence that would shock them if they ever attempted to escape their pen. "They would have treated us as badly as animals," Alan says. Only intervention by the local government prevented this plan from going into action. But the public-relations damage had been done.

Until the 1990s, much of England's social elite treated the game with snobbish disdain. Before Rupert Murdoch tried to acquire Manchester United, his paper the *Sunday Times* famously branded soccer "a slum sport played by slum people." Britain's prime minister Margaret Thatcher, the leading proponent of middle-class values soi-disant, exhibited this haughtiness as much as anyone. The Iron Lady's good friend Kenneth Clark said that she "regarded football supporters as the enemy within." For much of her tenure, she spoke aloud of her desire to declare war on hooliganism. And in 1989, her government had the ideal pretext for taking action. At the Hillsborough Stadium in Sheffield, ninety-five fans watching Liverpool play Nottingham Forest were asphyxiated against the fences in the over-crowded terraces that held them. In response to this carnage, a government commission demanded that stadiums turn their standing-only terraces into proper seats, like the ones you might find at a theater. Policing at stadiums would finally become a serious business, with video cameras documenting every fight and song.

The new requirements transformed the game's economics. To finance the reconstruction of their stadiums, the old owners, mostly small self-made businessmen, imported loads of new capital. Much of it came from slick city investors, who understood that soccer held a giant captive market and massive untapped profit centers. The new stands included plush executive suites that they leased to corporations. They floated shares of their clubs on the stock exchange, raised ticket prices, and sold the league's television rights to Rupert Murdoch's satellite service. Their plan worked to perfection. A new, wealthier fan began attending games in the safer, more comfortable stadiums. For the first time, women were plentiful in the stands.

But these changes came at a cost. The new clientele eroded the old, boisterous working-class ambience. As Alan explained this transformation, he invoked a time when "ten thousand would come to the stadium. Six thousand of them would be up for a fight. The rest came to watch a fight. Yeah, they'd say they were disgusted. But you'd ask them in the pub afterwards, 'Did you watch the fight or the football?' " He leans back and imitates a prig's voice, " 'Oh, the fight, of course.' " He laughs at his own observation. "Now, people just want to go to the game so that they can say"—he reverts to the prig persona—" 'Look, I'm cool. I go to Chelsea.' When I get up to sing, they say, 'Sit down.' "

Unwittingly, Alan boiled down the essential cultural argument against globalization made by *No Logo* author Naomi Klein, the McDonald's-smashing French farmer José Bove, and countless others: multinational capitalism strips local institutions of their localness, it homogenizes, destroys traditions, and deprives indigenous proletariats and peasants of the things they love most. It's easy to understand how this argument would apply

to English soccer in general and Chelsea in particular.
When I attended a game at the Stamford Bridge, I went
with an American investment banker and his Latin
American girlfriend. We sat in part of the stadium that
Alan Garrison had once ruled with his band of rowdies.
But in comparison to the taunting songsters of Glasgow, Chelsea looked like the audience at a symphony,
with only a few beefy guys muttering incendiary
obscenities under their breaths. They studiously kept
their vulgarities to themselves, so that police scanning
the crowd with handheld cameras would see nothing
and have no basis for depriving them of their tickets.
(Alan has lost his three times.)

But it's possible to overstate the change and the
case against change. For starters, the game hasn't gone
completely yuppie. Sure, ticket prices may be high at
Chelsea—about $50 for a seat—but they're not prohib-
itively expensive. Even in posh West London, perhaps
the most yuppie stretch in the whole of Britain, Chelsea
still manages to draw a largely working-class crowd.
The main difference is that it's an integrated crowd,
labor and management, street cleaner and advertising
executive together. In the course of English history, this
may be an earth-shattering development.

In response to the rise of corporate power, there's a
natural inclination to believe that self-interest hadn't
always ruled the market. Soccer writers in England
often portray the old club owners as far more
beneficent, public-minded citizens doing good for their
old working-class friends. But this is nostalgia for a
social market that never existed. Before the nineties,
there was so little money in the game that owners let

their stadiums decay into reprehensible safety traps. In effect, owners treated their fans as if their lives were expendable. Their negligence resulted in a complete breakdown, the broken-windows theory of social decay in microcosm. Fans began to think of life as expendable, too. They would beat the crap out of one another each weekend. To be sorrowful about the disappearance of this old culture requires grossly sentimentalizing the traditions and atmosphere that have passed. Indeed, this is an important characteristic of the globalization debate: the tendency toward glorifying all things indigenous, even when they deserve to be left in the past. So, in a way, a hooligan's nostalgia for his youth is the most honest kind of nostalgia.

III.

Before I met Alan Garrison, I had dipped into his writings. Surfing Chelsea Web sites, I had stumbled upon a page maintained by Alan plugging excerpts from *We're the North Stand,* an unpublished novelized memoir of his early days as a hooligan. It is a picaresque work about a circle of friends who travel England and Europe picking fights. In the manuscript, he refers to himself as Alan Merrill—a nom de plume which separates him further from his nom de guerre which separates him from any self-incriminating admissions.

Garrison writes with surprising clarity and panache. But as a novelist, he has a few shortcomings. The Merrill character has an unbelievable streak of heroic self-sacrificing interventions that remove innocent bystanders from harm. He wins fights like a superhero disposing of common criminals. ("One [hooligan] throws a desperate punch back towards Merrill, who ducks it easily before grabbing hold of the extended wrist. He then quickly pulls the youth around, using himself as the pivot-point, sending the helpless body crashing into the gate's upright.") Still, in many ways, it's an astonishing bit of self-sociology. Garrison doesn't try to elevate his friends into rebels pursuing a higher cause or monsters acting out the pathologies of poverty. They are simply average guys stuck in a world of violence from which they don't have any particular desire to escape.

Garrison is the thinking man's hooligan, a careful reader of military history and newspapers and a devoted Hellenist, who spends his free time poring over works on Alexander the Great. He doesn't admit it, but it must have irked him that he hadn't thought of writing a memoir earlier. By the time he put pen to paper, three of his friends had already sent off manuscripts to publishers. Steve "Hickey" Hickmont, who assumed Alan's place in the Chelsea hierarchy during his prison years, had published *Armed for the Match*. His buddy Chris "Chubby" Henderson wrote another memoir. Yet another comrade called Martin King hit the shelves with *Hoolifan,* a different perspective on the same tale. Convinced that he had his own crackling version to tell, Garrison sent his manuscript to his friends' publishers. Where his friends had worked with coauthors, Garrison wrote his by himself. Perhaps he hoped that the authenticity of his unadulterated voice would provide his competitive advantage. It didn't. He received polite rejections—the only way really to reject a hooligan. "They told me that the book was too violent and right-wing."

If they were honest, however, the publishers would have given him another explanation. The market simply couldn't sustain another memoir about hooliganism—or at least it shouldn't. Aside from the Chelsea books, hooligans from West Ham's Inter City Firm, Cardiff City's Soul Crew, Portsmouth's 657 Crew, and virtually every other major and minor club have produced their own tediously repetitive memoirs, with such titles as *Want Some Aggro?* and *City Psychos.* These days, the sports section at corner London bookshops largely consists of this hooligan lit. The genre goes far beyond these first-person tales. Two brothers called Dougie and Eddy Brimson, whose dust jacket shows them with appropriately shaved heads and comically attempting menacing gazes, have made a franchise of publishing pop anthropological studies of soccer violence. Their books quote heavily from hooligans and have names like *Eurotrashed* and *Capital Punishment: London's Violent Football Following.* A novelist called John King has added a shelf full of hooligan fiction, mostly about Chelsea. Another shelf includes books on hooligan fashion and the underground hooligan economy, as well as tomes by academics hoping to cash in on their sexy specialization.

On a smaller scale, the English hooligan has become like the gangsta rapper or the Mafioso, a glamorized, commodified criminal. When the BBC finds itself in need of a ratings boost, it airs one of its many hooligan documentaries. Every month, it seems, one of the British men's magazines rolls out a piece documenting some new wrinkle of domestic hooliganism or its foreign offspring. The full breadth of this phenomenon hadn't struck me until I went to see Chelsea in person. Walking down Fulham Road, I came across a vendor laying out tables with a collection of hats and pins bearing the skull-and-bones symbol of the infamous Headhunters gang. In the stands, I saw one teen with spiky hair wearing a blue Headhunters T-shirt. Stadium security must have felt comfortable letting him through the gates, knowing that no true hooligan would be dumb enough to flash them such an advertisement.

This hooligan industry only started in the late nineties, when the gentrification of the English game was already in full swing, at a point when hooliganism had ceased to flourish in its traditional form. Of course, hooligans still fought, just not inside the stadium. As Alan explained the mechanics of fighting to me, "You call up the leader of the other firm and say, 'Right, meet you at Trafalgar Square at two.' And then you hope that the police don't get there before it goes off. Sometimes it goes off. Sometimes you see the coppers and walk away." For Alan, this new mode of appointment hooliganism trampled the pleasure of pure art. It was far more exhilarating when fights took place in narrow corridors of stadiums or in the stands. And with all the prearrangement, "fighting has lost it spontaneity." He poses the existential question of the modern soccer hooligan: "If football violence doesn't take place in the stadium, is it even football violence?" Even though it pains him to admit it, he believes that hooliganism has been domesticated, or domesticated enough to become an object of fascination and adoration.

You can understand why the market might have an appetite for the hooligan. On the most basic level, he's a romantic rebel, willing to risk bodily harm and battle police. He's not just a nihilist. He fights for the colors of the club, the same colors that the average peace-abiding fan loves. Because the hooligan is so similar, he is so fascinating. Why would some fans—guys who are part of liberal, peaceful England—take full leave of conventional morality and become thugs?

The hooligan literature doesn't try to answer this question analytically. The mode is confessional and it aims to shock. (To quote at random from Alan's work, "The body fall[s] face downward on the platform, blood gushing from a deep cut in the back of the skull.") Nevertheless, the authors feel the need to justify their violent behavior. They may have left conventional morality, but they still live near it. The hooligans typically describe themselves as practicing a virtuous violence: They never assault innocent bystanders, and they never use weapons. Too often, the desire to self-exculpate combines with the narrative imperative to shock to produce comic book writing, all bams and splats.

Garrison, like all the rest, sanitizes the story, omitting some of the most interesting biographical details. That's too bad, because it's quite a story. From his early days as a Chelsea hooligan, he had become a self-admitted addict of the violence and the adrenaline that precedes it. "Fear is a drug," he says, "There's a very thin line between being hero and coward. It's better than sex. It lasts longer as well." He decided that he wanted a career that would deliver the rush in regular doses. After school, with London in full swinging sixties mode, he bucked the emerging hippie zeitgeist and enlisted in the army. More specifically, he volunteered for a unit in the elite special services that would give him the most opportunities to practice his beloved craft of violence.

Alan began living a strange double life. During the week, and for long stretches of the year, he would serve his country. At times, this would involve taking part in secret missions to fight and train armies whose identity he's reluctant to divulge. On weekends, he returned to his teenage football fighting. He reckons that the army knew about his double life—how could they not, with such a long sheet of crimes?—but didn't much care about any weekend havoc so long as he performed his weekday duties. As part of this double life, he began acquiring the trappings of conventionality. He married and had a daughter. Although his wife would plead with him to cut out the violence, she had no leverage to push her case. By the time they first met, "she'd heard about me from a friend who'd worked with her. We met at an office Christmas party. I introduced myself to her and she said, 'I don't want to know you. You're a fucking hooligan.' " She could never accuse Alan of selling her a false bill of goods.

His two lives fed off one another. "I was trained to fight and I couldn't turn it off," he says. His other comrades didn't want to turn it off either. Garrison says eight fellow soldiers joined him in the hooligan ranks. They brought a measure of professionalism to the fight. On a trip to the States, Garrison smuggled back CB radios, then illegal in Britain, and used them to coordinate assaults. The hooligan soldiers would carefully map out stadiums and their surroundings. Alan would stand back from the fray and track proceedings using binoculars and radio reports. "We were the fire brigade. When someone got into trouble, needed some help, we would come in and sort things out."

But there was tension between his existences, and in 1977, they ceased to be compatible. Chelsea traveled to the southwest of the country for a match at Plymouth. As the game ended, Garrison and his friends began bullying their way into the section holding Plymouth fans. Garrison had settled into combat with an opponent when, without his ever seeing it coming, an iron pipe made solid, shattering contact with the back of his skull. The furtive attacker struck him on the hand, too. Unfortunately for the attacker, he failed to knock the consciousness out of Garrison, who rose to his feet, seized the pipe, and began extracting vengeance. A blow to the face knocked his adversary's eye from the socket. "It was hanging by a string," he admits. It was Garrison's ill fortune that a police officer entered the scene at this moment, with the eye and pipe weighing heavily against Alan's protestations of innocence.

When he came to trial, Garrison supplied the court with x-rays of his broken hand and fractured skull to prove that he had acted in self-defense. This evidence, however, couldn't overcome the eyewitness account of a cop. A judge sent Garrison away for attempted murder. He left his family to spend nearly five years in Dartmoor prison.

IV.

On my next trip to London, Garrison met me at the
Finchley Road tube stop near his home. We walked
down the street for a drink at Weatherspoon's Pub.
When I took out my wallet to buy drinks, he pushed it
away.

"I'm Jewish, but not that Jewish. You bought last
time."

Alan wore a T-shirt with air-brushed scorpions that
he had purchased at a market near San Francisco a few
years ago. He told me, "Bought it for seventy-five dollars off the artist. I later found out that was quite a good
deal."

Conversations with Garrison invariably lead back to
the Bay Area. In the eighties, after his release from
prison, he fell into a career as a graphics designer, with
a specialty in video games. When one of his friends
landed in Silicon Valley, just in time for the dot-com
boom of the nineties, Alan followed him to California.
Miraculously, the Immigration and Naturalization Service overlooked his convictions and granted Alan a
work visa. He bought himself a house in the San Francisco suburbs.

"So what was the dot-com boom like?" I asked.

He paused uncharacteristically to think it over and
then responded with a non sequitur. "Jesus Christ, but
the women out there are sharks. Sitting at a bar, they're
around you like flies to shit. One day I was chatting
with one bird and she says, 'Are you coming back to my
place?' Then she got into her purse and pulled out this
thing. 'This is my AIDS certificate. I've been tested.'

And I'm like what? She says, 'I've been tested.' I said, 'When was that?' She said, 'Three weeks ago.' And I said, 'How many blokes have you been with since then? Fuck off.'" He waved his hand, laughing at his story. "Women out there are like sharks, especially around English accents."

In his book, he constantly flashes to scenes from his life in California and juxtaposes them with life in England. It makes for quite a contrast. But Alan also credits himself with bridging cultural gaps. The first time we met, he wore an Oakland Raiders jacket. It was an entirely appropriate outfit. Of all American football clubs, the Raiders have a reputation for surly, working-class fans that most closely approximate English soccer hooligans. During his years as an American, Garrison supported the Raiders as fervently as he could support any organization that wasn't Chelsea. "We tried to teach them how to behave like proper hooligans," told me. At a game in San Diego, he organized Raiders fans to make "a run" through the parking lot, throwing punches and asserting dominance over the home crowd that stood turning hot dogs on their portable grills. "They didn't know what hit them."

Liberal northern California is hardly a place fit for a Chelsea hooligan. More than any club, Chelsea has been associated with the neo-Nazi right. I had just seen a BBC documentary that showed how many of the Chelsea hooligans—people that Alan knows—travel to concentration camps on tourist trips so that they can admire Hitler's accomplishments. They deliver *sieg heil* salutes to the tourists and confiscate artifacts for their personal collections of concentration camp paraphernalia. Back in London, they've provided protection for Holocaust denier David Irving.

This history of English hooliganism can best be told as a distorted version of mainstream youth culture. At first, in Alan's heyday, hooliganism imitated the early "I Want to Hold Your Hand" Beatles' nonpolitical rebellion. It was all a good laugh, just for fun. Then, in the seventies, hooliganism began to dabble in radical politics. Only, as practitioners of hate and violence, they couldn't credibly join with the peace-love-dope crowd. They went in the opposite direction, becoming the vanguard of the proto-fascist British nationalist movement. And just as the youth movement veered toward mindlessness, nihilism, and punk, the Chelsea movement became even more mindless, nihilist, and punk. During Alan's imprisonment, admiration for the Nazis became a virtue.

As their numbers grew, Chelsea hooligans began subdividing into groups called "firms." The most famous of the groups called themselves the Chelsea Headhunters. After their assaults, they would leave a calling card with their skull-and-bones logo that read, "You have been nominated and dealt with by the Chelsea Headhunters." In addition to linking up with the far right, the Headhunters joined with criminal elements. They began peddling drugs and used other criminal rackets to become quite rich. Like the Bloods and Crips of L.A. street gang fame, they spent their money on fancy cars and designer clothes.

Another group formed a coalition of hooligans across teams called Combat 18. It derived its moniker from a numerological breakdown of Adolf Hitler's name, with the A yielding the 1 and H being the eighth letter of the alphabet. Originally, the group began as a security force for the racialist British National Party, which had some horrifying luck exploiting xenophobia for electoral gain. But in the early nineties Combat 18 grew disillusioned with the softness of the BNP, even though the party unabashedly admired the Nazis. Combat 18 had no patience with the BNP's reformist embrace of electoral politics. They wanted White Revolution and they exploded nail bombs in immigrant neighborhoods, instigated race riots in Oldham, and plotted to kidnap the left-wing actress Vanessa Redgrave.

Although Alan identified himself as a right winger, he also presented his own politics as reasonably mainstream. Most of his judgments could have been issued by any conservative pundit on a TV chat show. But he also obviously hailed from the Combat 18 milieu. Many of the hard core from the terrorist right shared his demographic profile precisely. A slew of these thugs had even served in the special services, like Alan, before the police caught up with them. So I asked, "What about Combat 18?"

Occasionally, on these sensitive subjects, Alan would tell me to turn off my tape recorder and put down my pen. But, this time, he didn't. He shifted his glass of Coke to the side. "First, this whole racist thing is bullshit. They're nationalists. There are blacks in Combat 18. . . . That's what I mean about this whole racist thing: It's bullshit. If someone comes here [to England] like Kojak," a black Chelsea hooligan, "he considers himself English. He talks with an English accent. He says, 'I'm brought up here. I'm English. I don't give a toss if my parents came from the West Indies.' He'll fight for anything English. And he's in Combat 18, which is right wing. It's not racist right wing. It's nationalist right wing." He was adamant about this point.

"And what about the Jews? What about the Yids at Tottenham? Does that bother you?"

"Nobody bothers me. They make jokes, but I joke about being Jewish myself."

While he spoke, I thought of the documentary I had seen the night before: the image of Chelsea hooligans sending postcards from Auschwitz to an anti-fascist activist back in England: "Wish you were here so that you could see me pissing on your mother's bones."

V.

The new economy may not have survived the nineties, but it left behind a new profession: the consultant. Every industry has them. Why should hooliganism be any different? While Alan doesn't fight regularly, he and the other semiretired Chelsea hooligans advise and mentor a group of teens that calls itself the Youth Firm. "We help them plan. And when it goes off, we stay back with a map and mobile phone." The old hooligans keep a hand in the youngsters' operation, because they're loath to give up all the pleasures of battle—and filled with nostalgia for their own youths. They also feel a sense of obligation to the institution that has nurtured them for so long. "We feel a certain responsibility to the young guys," Alan told me. "We want them to succeed. They're Chelsea. And we have experience that can be helpful to them."

Like a college alumni association, the semiretired hooligans make a point of sticking together. They stay in touch through a message board, where they discuss the Youth Firm, exchange war stories and opinions about their beloved club. Not surprisingly, for a group that longs for the past, a large number of their posts concern their portrayal in the memoirs published by their fellow hooligans. They're especially sensitive to the depictions of Chelsea in the books written by gangs from rival clubs. Responding to a memoir by a Hull City hooligan, a fellow with the handle "monkeyhanger" dismisses the bravura of the book's authors: "[B]unch ov shity arse we took over there town, they stayed in there little pub the silver cod where were they were safe . . . as for the book we'll say no more. toilet paper springs to mind." After reading a West Ham United memoir, one respondent inveighs, "Pure Fiction! The Only Way They'll Be Doin Chelsea."

When the Russian-Jewish oil baron Roman Abramovich bought Chelsea, I jumped online to gauge reactions on their message board—and to see if Garrison would weigh in. The board makes a point of declaring, "Welcome to the Chelsea Hooligan Message Board, This Board is Not Here for the Purpose of Organizing Violence or Racist Comment." Needless to say, this warning doesn't exactly deter the anti-Semitism. Almost immediately after the Abramovich purchase, a guy named West Ken Ken moaned, "I like the money but the star of david will be flying down the [Stamford] bridge soon." The title of his post is, "Not much said about Roman being a yid." A few scattered comments endorsed West Ken Ken's sentiments. Considering some of the attacks on Tottenham that come from his mouth, it is somewhat surprising that Garrison should be sensitive to West Ken Ken's burst of Jew hating. But he is. Garrison appeared on the board and presented West Ken Ken with a stern, pedantic reprimand: "Being a Yeed means you support that shit from [Tottenham]. Totally different form [sic] being a Jew, you know the ones that kick the shit out of Muslims." It's a brilliant response. He invokes the idea of *Muskeljudentum,* of the ass-kicking Israeli, to defend his people on a hooligan's own terms. And the only reply to Garrison that can be mustered is, "Yes, I forgot you are one of the chosen race."

How much violence does Alan still cause? Alan says he has launched a second career as a soldier of fortune, working for a German company that hires out mercenaries. He mentioned his work in Croatia and Kosovo. On his last trip to the Balkans, he had told his wife that he was just going to train soldiers, not to fight. "She thought I was too old and out of shape to be doing this anymore." But when he returned, he and his wife were sitting at home, flipping channels. They came across a documentary on the Kosovo war. The opening scene showed Alan in mid-battle. "She wasn't too pleased with me that evening."

Those days of fighting are probably all in the past now. But Alan claims that he hasn't fully retired from hooliganism. About four times a year, usually after games against Tottenham, he says that he goes out and throws a few punches. I wasn't sure whether to believe him. The best way to judge, I thought, would be to watch him in his natural habitat. I wanted to see how close he was to the active hooligans.

On game day, I found Alan and his friends at a bar in the second story of a shopping mall not far from Stamford Bridge. Alan drank a Coke and hovered over a table. He introduced me to his best friend Angus, and reminded me of his appearances in his book. Angus had brought along his twenty-something daughter. The three of them laughed at dirty jokes that Angus received via text message on his cell phone. To the side, there was a table filled with Alan's other friends. Only Angus's daughter wore a jersey. "We prefer not to identify ourselves. We like to be able to mix with the crowd," Alan said.

But, based on their behavior and looks, these characters didn't appear to be active goons. In fact, they didn't seem like they had often risen from their couches, let alone recently kneed violent sociopaths in the testicles.

I told Alan that I had spotted fans of Manchester City, that weekend's opposing club, at a pub down the street. "They were just sitting outside drinking. Are they allowed to do that? Will nobody give them a hard time?" I described the facade of the pub to Alan.

"That's a Chelsea pub," he told me.

He turned away and told one of his friends, "Frank

says that there were City fans down the street. They were in a Chelsea pub. That's not right." His tone was outrage.

His friend looked up from his table at me. He had been collecting cash from friends to rent a van that would travel to Liverpool for next week's game. "Alan would still have a go. If Tottenham were here, he might even throw a punch." He rolled his eyes. Besides, even if they weren't too old to do it, they still wouldn't be crazy enough to put themselves in that kind of situation, fighting so close to the stadium. That style of battle is a distant memory. Too many police hover outside the pubs.

Alan and I walked across the room to Angus and his daughter. Angus was now a bit drunk and the bar's bouncer was trying to steer him into a seat, where he wouldn't stumble into the path of waiters.

Angus began telling a story about traveling to Nottingham Forest, "It was just the two of us and two of them. The police saw us coming up against one another. And they thought it was funny. They were laughing their fuckin' asses off. They just let us have a go at one another. Of course, this guy here," he pointed to Alan. "He got to go against the little twat. I took this enormous bloke." He mimed a man flexing his muscles. "I jumped on 'im and bit his ear off."

He turned to his daughter, doubled over in laughter, and then finished telling his tale.

"Them were the days," Alan said. And so they went on, rendering each story with manic intensity and scenes of incredible drama.

A few minutes later we began to walk to the game

with the crowd. As we went down an escalator, Alan pulled up his pants leg to reveal a cowboy boot with a steel tip. "Good for giving a kicking."

As he disembarked, sloppy drunk Angus leaned over to me and whispered, "But when was the last time they were used for kicking?"

5

How Soccer Explains
the Survival of the Top Hats

I.

When players score goals at Rio's São Januário stadium, they have visions of the crucifixion. Less than twenty yards behind the goalkeeper's net, a dark wooden cross bulges forth from the stained glass of a mid-century-modernist chapel, Our Lady of Victories. A few yards to the left, in the sight line of corner kicks, a small garden is filled with pedestals displaying concrete statuettes of the Madonna and other icons. This is how the world expects the game to be played in Brazil, the cradle of soccer civilization: transcendently.

São Januário belongs to the club Vasco da Gama, and the stadium is itself a shrine to Brazilian soccer. Throughout the club's storied history, its players have perfectly embodied Rio de Janeiro's Dionysian temperament—like Romario, the star of the 1994 World Cup. He compensates for his undisguised distaste for running with his gift for deception. Long ago, every Rio journalist tells me, his coaches stopped pleading with him to leave the beach, to come away from his bar, and join the squad on the training ground.

In 2002, Romario ditched Vasco for a cross-town rival. Since his departure, the most iconic figure at São Januário is no longer a player. You can see his visage just above Our Lady of Victories, on a large billboard that hangs from a tower adjoining the field. It's the unsmiling face of a balding, gray-haired, multichinned man with sizeable gold-rimmed glasses. His name is Eurico Miranda, a federal congressman and the president of Vasco da Gama. The billboard trumpets him as a "symbol of resistance." When I visit São Januário, the symbol is everywhere. Signs for his reelection—"a voice against the powerful"—ring the outside of the stadium. Across the street from São Januário's main gate, a Ford Escort with a loudspeaker mounted on its roof plays a samba tune that proclaims, "Eurico is the candidate of the poor people." Entering the stadium, an unavoidable banner in midfield exclaims, "Passion for Vasco, Devotion to Eurico."

Americans call their sporting teams "franchises." Brazilians would never tolerate that use of the term. It has too many commercial associations with chains of McDonald's and dry cleaners. Instead, Brazilians call their teams "clubs," because most are actually clubs. They have swimming pools, restaurants, tennis courts, palm-covered gardens, and dues-paying members— places for the middle class to spend a Saturday afternoon. Even though the clubs pay their players, they have retained their status as nonprofit amateur enterprises. This means that their finances are not subjected to public scrutiny; their executives have no legal accountability. In short, their management ranks make the perfect refuge for scoundrels. These scoundrels have grown so integral to the Brazilian game that everyone calls them by their nickname, the *cartolas*, the top hats. As part of the amateur structure of the game, the *cartolas* usually receive no salary. They supposedly toil for their gentlemanly love of their club. In practice, however, the *cartolas* reward their volunteer efforts with dips into the team treasury. João Havelange, the legendary ex-president of the Brazilian Soccer Confederation (CBF) and former boss of international soccer's governing body (FIFA), once remarked, "I take no salary, just enough expenses to get by on."

When Eurico Miranda joined Vasco's management in 1975, in his early thirties, he'd been a man of limited means. The son of a Portuguese baker, he'd worked as a salesman at a Rio Volkswagen dealership. But with his charisma, he quickly politicked his way up the Vasco hierarchy. It changed his life. He acquired oceanside houses in Rio and a yacht. This is not a tale of wealth earned with up-by-the-bootstraps industry. By now, the Brazilian press and a congressional investigation have documented Miranda's offenses. In 1998, Vasco received $34 million in cash from NationsBank (now Bank of America), eager to establish a name for itself in the vast Brazilian market by sponsoring a popular sporting brand. When the bank signed the deal, it announced that the cash would last the club for 100 years. Within two, however, this supply had more or less vanished. Approximately $124,000 worth had gone to buy T-shirts and propaganda for Eurico Miranda's last election campaign. Twelve million went to four accounts of a Bahamas company called Liberal Banking Corporation Limited. As it turned out, the company was very liberal. Any legal representative of Vasco could withdraw the money. According to a report published by the Brazilian senate, the withdrawn money ended up as payments to Miranda's car dealer, business investments, credit card company, brother, and Internet provider. "It is clear," the senate concluded, "Mr. Miranda has diverted to his accounts money that belonged to Vasco." Miranda hadn't covered his trail very carefully. He didn't need to. As long as he held on to his congressional seat, parliamentary immunity protected him from prosecution. With the support of Vasco's many voting fans, he looked like he could hang on forever.

But because Miranda squandered the Bank of America investment, Vasco has slid into debt and mediocrity. In 1998, it won the Latin American championship, the Copa Libertadores. Three years later, the club owed its star player Romario $6.6 million in back wages. Worse than that, to keep enough players on the pitch, Romario reportedly had to dig into his own accounts to cover the weekly paychecks of his teammates. Desperate for extra cash, Vasco packed fans into São Januário for big games. In the last game of 2000, Vasco management crammed in more than 12,000 over the maximum seating capacity. After a brawl ignited in the stands, fans began fleeing and then falling on one another. They cascaded toward the pitch, their downward flow stanched only by a rusty fence. When the fence collapsed, the crowd came tumbling down onto the field. There were 168 casualties. Any decent person would have canceled the match as soon as the injured bodies began stacking on the pitch and helicopters hauled them away. Miranda insisted that the game go on.

II.

Based on the stylishness of Brazil's 2002 World Cup triumph—Edmilson springing backwards, catapult-like, into a poster-quality bicycle kick; Ronaldo scoring in-stride with a poke of the toe—you'd have no conception of the crisis in the national passion. But Brazilian soccer couldn't be in a sorrier state—no more corrupt, no more discouraging to fans, no more unappealing to investors. Only a handful of clubs operate in the vicinity of the black. In 2002, Flamengo of Rio de Janeiro, easily the most popular club in the nation, owed creditors over $100 million, an incomprehensible sum in the stunted Brazilian economy. You can see the signs of decay everywhere. Attending games in some of the country's most storied stadiums, buying their most expensive tickets, I found myself worrying about splinters and rusty nails protruding from the rotting wooden seats.

Usually, such woeful conditions are attributable to poverty. The Brazilian game, however, has hardly starved for capital. In fact, there was an international, well-monied venture to raise the Brazilian game to a Western European standard of quality. In 1999, a Dallas-based investment fund called Hicks, Muse, Tate & Furst sank millions into the São Paulo club Corinthians and into the Belo Horizonte club Cruzeiro. ISL, a Swiss sports marketing firm, acquired a share of Flamengo. A few years earlier, the Italian food giant Parmalat began running Palmeiras of São Paulo. These investors came implicitly promising to wipe away the practices of corrupt *cartolas* and replace them with the ethic of professionalism, the science of modern marketing, and a concern for the balance sheet. "Capitalism is winning out against the feudal attitudes that have prevailed in the sport for too long," Brazil's venerable soccer journalist Juca Kfouri crowed at the height of the foreign influx. Newspapers carried their predictions that soccer would generate four percent of Brazil's gross domestic product within years.

When the investors talked about exploiting the potential of Brazilian soccer, they wanted to capitalize on a single fact of the game: The Brazilian style is so much more aesthetically pleasing than any other brand of play. In the postwar years, when international competition truly began, Brazil became an international power because it played without the rigid strategic strictures of continental soccer. Positions, formations, and defense weren't valued nearly so much as spontaneity, cleverness, and the scoring of goals. To paraphrase the Italian film director Pier Paolo Pasolini's formulation, where the European style was prose, the Brazilian was poetry. The Brazilians created a whole new set of conventions for the game: passes with the back of the heel, an array of head and hip fakes, the bicycle kick.

But while the Brazilian style and some Brazilian players have flourished in the global economy, Brazil has not. Across the world, sport isn't renowned for its strenuous ethics. But the *cartolas* are a special breed. Every time a rising superstar becomes a fan favorite, he's sold to Europe. It's not just the greedy chasing of paychecks. A substantial number of Brazilians prefer unglamorous leagues in the Faeroe Islands, Haiti, and Albania to remaining at home. They're fleeing the capricious rule of the *cartolas,* who overhaul the rules for the Brazilian championship annually—usually to benefit the most politically powerful clubs. As Ronaldo told reporters in 1998, "I wouldn't return to Brazil now for any offer."

Despite their ambitions and resources, foreign investors did nothing to change this. Less than three years after the foreign investors arrived, they left in disgrace. At Corinthians, fans held demonstrations against Hicks, Muse, protesting its failure to deliver on grand promises to buy superstars and build a modern stadium. At Flamengo, ISL collapsed into bankruptcy. Foreign capital hadn't turned Brazilian soccer into the NBA of global soccer or rid the game of corruption. In fact, by many objective measures, the game is now in worse shape than when they arrived. So this is more than a tragic tale of sporting decline; it's an example of how the bad parts of globalization can undermine the good ones; this is the story of how corruption beats back liberalization and turns Thomas Friedman on his head.

III.

As with any story about Brazilian soccer, there's a natural place to begin: the king, by which I mean Edson Arantes do Nascimento, by which I mean, of course, Pelé. He's the natural starting place because he is a cen-

tral character in the globalization of Brazilian soccer, and
the struggle to salvage the game from the ruinous rule
of the *cartolas*. But he also makes a good starting place,
because his biography is the economic history of Brazil.

It begins in 1940 on the frontier west of Rio, in an
impoverished town called Tres Coracoes. With his slight
frame (145 pounds at the start of his career), Edson
Arantes's body seemed more suited to shoe shining
and the resale of tobacco gathered from discarded cigarettes, his first vocations. But he had a pushy father,
Dondinho, whose own aspirations to soccer greatness
and social mobility ended with the ripping of right knee
ligaments in his first and only professional appearance.
From the start, it was clear Dondinho had quite a target
to push. Despite his physical limitations, Pelé possessed an uncanny ability to shoot from an impossible
angle, a manner of handling the ball that looked more
like a caress than a dribble, a charismatic style. By dint
of fluke injuries to his teammates, at age sixteen, he
started for the prestigious Santos Football Club in
Brazil's booming coffee port. At age seventeen, in 1958,
with a flick over the head of the Swedish keeper Anders
Svensson, he clinched his first World Cup.

Brazil is the bizarro version of the United States.
It's the fantastically vast, resource-rich, new-world
culture that didn't become a global hegemon. In
Pelé's prime, the fifties and sixties, Brazil made a self-
conscious choice to reverse this condition. First a series
of populist presidents (1956–1964), then the military
dictatorship (1964–1985), practiced an aggressive
brand of forced industrialization and economic nationalism, ratcheting up tariffs, opening state-run firms,

and ordering public works projects at a furious pace. "Fifty years in five" was the Soviet-ish slogan of president Juscelino Kubitschek's regime in the late fifties and early sixties. The pump had been primed. By end of Kubitschek's presidency in 1961, the country's GDP was growing at a pace of 11 percent per year.

Pelé became the regime's symbol of this boom, what economists called the "Brazilian Miracle"—evidence that Brazil could become an international power on its own terms, without plagiarizing from foreign models. By the seventies, the dictators plastered his face across billboards next to their slogans ("No one will hold Brazil back now!"). The military dictators played the theme song of Pelé's 1970 World Cup winning team at official events. Upon the team's return to Brazil, President Emilio Médici announced, "I identify this victory won in the brotherhood of good sportsmanship with the rise of faith in our national development."

Like his country, Pelé amassed a small fortune. His club, Santos, gave him a $125,000 salary, a Volkswagen, and a house for his parents. He'd become one of the best-paid athletes of his day. But the fortune never made him wealthy. Sycophants plundered his accounts. A Spanish agent called Pepe Gordo, introduced to Pelé in 1965 by a teammate, ran down Pelé's pile of cash with a string of dunderheaded investments in fly-by-night companies and undesirable real estate. (Instead of breaking with Pepe Gordo, or better yet suing him, Pelé made him the best man at his first wedding.) In another era, he would have quickly recovered his losses by signing with a rich European club. But in 1960, the government declared Pelé a "non-exportable national treasure."

Uneducated and unworldly, he didn't know better and never seemed to assimilate the lessons of his mistakes. So he repeated them. After Pelé retired in 1974, he trusted advisors who made him the unwitting guarantor of a massive loan that went bad. "Once again, after all the warnings and all the bad experience, I had signed something that I should not have signed," he wrote in his 1977 memoir. It was a very public humiliation. A year after retiring, amid sentimental goodbyes, he unretired to regain a little bit of his losses. He signed up with the New York Cosmos, a concoction of Warner Communications in the newly minted North American Soccer League, to play three seasons for $7 million.

His failings mirrored Brazil's own disastrous miscues. Like Pelé, the dictatorship attracted rogues who robbed the national treasury. And the mismanagement was worse than that. After the 1973 oil shocks, the military dictatorship insisted on keeping the economy aimed at the same spectacular growth rate. This meant even more state spending, which meant borrowing from foreign banks. Over the decade, the government built a $40 billion debt. This triggered a nightmarish chain— unable to get loans, the government could no longer fund industry; unable to fund industry, Brazil was slammed by unemployment. Inflation, sparked by state spending and then worsened by the new debt payments, compounded the poverty of the unemployed. By the end of the military dictatorship in 1985, Brazil suffered from the worst case of income inequality in the world.

For a time in the late '70s and early '80s, Pelé's trajectory diverged from Brazil's. With the Cosmos, he'd finally flourished financially. He told *Time* magazine in

2001 that America taught him that "[y]ou can't do business with members of your family. You can't appoint someone to be president of your company because he is a friend or your brother. You have to appoint the most capable person. Business is business. You have to be tough." Put differently, America made him a capitalist. In fact, it made him quite a good one. Even after his retirement, as the images of his triumphs faded, his profitability continued on a pace of almost exponential growth. He became the perfectly postmodern image, a brand backed by multinational companies. Pelé's figure now appears on two million MasterCards; Viagra, Nokia, Samsung, Coca-Cola, and Petrobras have tapped him as their international spokesman. Every year, he reportedly pockets more than $20 million from sponsorships alone.

It's tempting to view Pelé, with his up-from-the-favela tale and his terminally affable demeanor, as the Brazilian Steppinfetchit, the ideally inoffensive corporate spokesman. But this sells Pelé and his ambitions short. He wanted to build his own Brazilian version of Warner Communications. In 1993, Pelé set out to buy the broadcast rights for Brazil's national championship from the Brazilian Soccer Confederation (CBF). As the man most associated with the success of Brazilian soccer, he felt sure that he would be rewarded for his lifetime of contributions. And to ensure his position, he put cash behind his effort—$1 million more than his nearest competitor. But from his many years as a member of the national team, he should have grasped that market forces don't exactly govern CBF. One of the federation's apparatchiks demanded that Pelé send $1 million to a Swiss bank account for the right to have his bid reviewed by CBF. Pelé refused and lost the contract.

Bitter and humiliated, Pelé set out for revenge. He exposed the bribe in an interview with *Playboy*. Pelé couldn't have picked a juicier target. CBF's president, Ricardo Teixeira, perfectly embodied the decrepitude of the *cartolas*. An obscure lawyer, without any prior involvement in soccer or sports administration, he'd arrived at the highly prized position in the Brazilian game for a perfectly predictable reason: His father-in-law was João Havelange, then the all-powerful head of the international soccer federation. Over his tenure, he acquired increasingly fancy cars, an apartment in Miami, and an entourage of bodyguards. While CBF ran up massive debts, Teixeira's salary increased by more than 300 percent. Charges of corruption tailed him everywhere. Prosecutors busted him cold for tax evasion, although they couldn't beat out the statute of limitations.

For the few anti-corruption crusaders, it seemed their savior had finally arrived. Rich beyond imagination, they reasoned, Pelé could afford to speak truth to power. He had, after all, been a corporate mascot with morals, refusing to advertise for cigarettes and alcohol. "I only put my name to things I believe in," he liked to tell reporters. High-mindedness had always been part of Pelé's persona. When he scored his thousandth goal at Rio's Maracanã stadium in 1969, reporters rushed to ask his thoughts. He bellowed, "Remember the children, never forget Brazil's poor children."

Pelé's criticism of Teixeira fit the times. Latin America was in the midst of profound transformation—a broader revolt against corruption. After decades of protectionism and inflation, it was ready to ditch the crony capitalist style of the military dictators. In its place, it chose (at least its elites chose) neo-liberalism of the Washington school. At the vanguard of the change resided the sociologist Fernando Henrique Cardoso. He made an unlikely capitalist and a charmingly tweedy politician. During the '70s, he'd written the defining text of the Brazilian left, *Dependency and Development in Latin America.* His criticisms of the military government earned him interrogations, jail time, the firebombing of his office, and sporadic stints in exile. But without the military dictatorship as a foil, after the regime's collapse in 1985, Cardoso became ever less radical. By the time he became president in 1994, he'd emerged as the vital center of Brazilian politics.

Watching Pelé pick his battle with the crony capitalists at CBF, Cardoso saw a kindred ideological spirit and an opportunity for gamy politics. He named Pelé his Extraordinary Minister of Sports, Brazil's first-ever black cabinet minister. "A symbol of Brazil that has come up from the roots ... that has triumphed," Cardoso crowed as he made the announcement. From the start, it was clear that Pelé had bought into the government's "modernization" agenda. A year into his term, he proposed the "Pelé Law," a set of IMF-like reforms for soccer, requiring clubs to operate as transparent capitalist ventures, with open books and accountable managers. It gave players the right to free agency, to abandon their clubs after their contracts ended. His aide Celso Grelet told me, "We thought at the time we'd bring business rationality and professionalism to the clubs." Pelé hoped the reforms would attract foreign investors who would remake "Brazilian football into the

NBA of the footballing world." In a generation, Pelé had gone from exploited third-world labor to authoritarian icon to neo-liberal acolyte.

IV.

Flying into Rio, looking west from the mountaintop Jesus that reigns over the city, you can see the most famous Brazilian building, Maracanã stadium. From the street, staring at its squat steel rim, the Maracanã doesn't look like it could hold over 200,000 people—as it did for the finals of the 1950 World Cup, the largest ever live audience for a soccer game. It doesn't even rise above its middle-class neighborhood. In the air, however, the magnitude of the Maracanã becomes clear. It's one big hole in the ground. It seems to have an endless supply of corners into which fans can be shoved. Ringing the field, separated from the action by a deep moat, rows of concrete slabs can accommodate 40,000 fans in addition to the layers of seats above.

The Maracanã, like a duomo, is filled with memorials to heroes, martyrs, and its patron saint, Pelé. It was here that he scored his thousandth goal on November 19, 1969. And it was here, in 1961, as a plaque at the stadium's entrance commemorates, that Pelé scored "the most beautiful goal ever." Collecting the ball in front of his own keeper, he traversed the length of the field. Without a pass, but many feints at passing, he juked his way past six separate defenders. The ball never really left his feet until he put it in the net. Like much of Pelé's highlight reel—the time he dribbled two circles around a Senegalese keeper, the eight goals he put past a top Rio club in a single game—it doesn't exist on film, only in fading memories and folklore.

The lure of the Maracanã's mythic past is so strong that three of Rio's four teams have made it their home stadium. On a perfect August night at the beginning of a new season, I came to watch one of these storied clubs, Botafogo. I had expected one of the great sporting experiences. And the entrance didn't disappoint. You walk past a stretch of polished granite sidewalk, like the one in front of Mann's Chinese Theater, with blocks dedicated to Brazil's greatest players, coaches, and sportswriters. Well before the portal to the arena it is possible to hear the samba cadence of the drums.

The chants and drumbeat originate in a corner of the arena, just to the side of the goal. This is the *curva,* as the Italians call it. Across much of the Latin world, the *curva* is the traditional congregation of the exuberant clubs of supporters. They vigorously wave flags, at least ten feet tall, with slogans expressing undying allegiance to their beloved team. They spend all week composing new songs that they will use to taunt their opponent and champion their favorite players.

The Maracanã provides all the emotion that a fan could desire, except for one thing: company. Aside from the diehards in the *curva,* and a few dozen fans accompanying the visiting team who've been sequestered in their own distant *curva,* for safety's sake, there's almost no one in the vast stadium. When the public address announcer lists the names of players, the echo in the stadium renders him incomprehensible. According to the figure thrown up on the scoreboard, a measly 4,000 have shown. This number is sadly typical: thousands more fans attend the average soccer game in Columbus, Ohio, and Dallas, Texas, than in the top flight of the Brazilian league.

After one spends a little time in Rio, the reasons for this sparseness become obvious. Ubiquitous surveillance cameras have largely stamped out the thievery that used to lurk through the stadium, but the surrounding neighborhood is a shooting gallery. Trips to the bathroom mean splashing through pools of urine. Often enough, the stench is apparent outside the bathrooms, too. Many Brazilian fans don't want to risk missing any action on the pitch by making the long haul to the head. Maracanã recently renovated its infrastructure, not just to comply with new safety regulations, but also to reverse the corrosive effects of urine on steel-reinforced concrete girders.

Perhaps the public could have suffered these indignities. But the rulers of the Brazilian game have committed sins beyond depriving fans of amenities. They have disorganized the game itself. Every year they concoct a different system for the league, a new calendar and formula for winning the championship. One season, revenue from ticket sales was factored into playoff qualification. Schedules become so cluttered with meaningless tournaments that players essentially never have an off-season.

A few seats away, at half-time of the Botafogo game, a man is reading a newspaper story about Ronaldo. According to the piece, Real Madrid is trying to buy the bucktoothed striker off Internazionale of Milan for $20 million. In Pelé's day, the greatest Brazilian players played in Brazil, and, therefore, Brazilian fans were treated to the greatest games on the planet. Now, even my most soccer mad friends in Brazil have a hard time naming the players on storied clubs like Botafogo. Of the twenty-two players who wore their country's radioactive yellow jerseys in the World Cup, only seven currently play in their home country. An estimated 5,000 Brazilians have contracts with foreign teams. The exodus of Brazilian soccer play is one of the great migrations of talent in recent history, the sports equivalent of the post-Soviet brain drain or the flight of intellectuals from war-torn African countries. Brazilian heroes have become something like the war in Chechnya—distant and foreign, extant only in rare appearances for the national team and the dispatches of stringers.

V.

Well before President Cardoso named him to his cabinet, Pelé had maintained a cozy relationship with power. During the military dictatorship, he didn't complain when the regime lifted his image for its propaganda. When asked about the generals' unwillingness to hold elections, he once replied that he considered Brazilians too stupid to vote. He'd even struck up a friendship with Henry Kissinger. The role of rebel and reformer hadn't come naturally to Pelé, and he could only sustain it for so long. After using his prestige to shove his raft of anti-corruption, pro-capitalist reforms, the Pelé Laws, down the congress's gullet in 1998, he resigned from the government, to return to his lucrative life as the smiling icon.

But without the force of Pelé behind the Pelé Laws, the soccer lobby recovered the upper hand. Pelé's laurels withered before he could rest upon them. Two years after his retirement, his opponents orchestrated legislation undoing the most important reforms before they fully took effect. The *cartolas* wouldn't have to keep open books or face legal accountability for their accounting antics. As always, corruption in Brazil proved remarkably resilient. When faced with this fact, it was as if Pelé resigned himself to the reign of the *cartolas*. In February 2001, Pelé staged a press conference with the tainted chief of Brazilian soccer, Ricardo Teixeira, in Rio. They'd joined together, in Pelé's words, in a "pact to save Brazilian soccer." Teixeira announced that Pelé would head a special commission charged with reorganizing the administration of the sport. He then kissed the king's ring. "I made a huge mistake by distancing myself from the nation's greatest idol. I am acknowledging my remorse and am counting on Pelé's nobility to accept my apologies." Then, in front of the cameras, for the front pages of the papers, Teixeira and Pelé embraced.

In truth, nothing could have further undermined Pelé's nobility. No longer was he the scourge of the *cartolas*. At the conference, he condemned the congressional investigation for destroying the prestige of the national game. He'd given Teixeira credibility at the moment congress was ready to drive the stake into the *cartolas*. José Trajano, a columnist for the sports daily *Lance!*, thundered, "The union of Pelé and Ricardo Teixeira is the biggest stab in the back that those of us fighting for ethics in sport could receive. . . . He has sold his soul to the devil."

After the embrace, anti-corruption crusaders turned on Pelé. Reform-minded journalists began reconsidering Pelé's tenure as sports minister. In retrospect, it was obvious that he had been less than idealistic. Pelé's business partner had written the bulk of the Pelé Laws. At the same time Pelé's business associates wrote the laws, they freely admitted that they hoped to profit from them. Pelé had displayed a troubling lack of ethical common sense in other ways, too. He'd advised foreign investors to direct their money into some of the most corrupt enterprises in Brazil. In 1998, for example, he helped broker the relationship between Eurico Miranda and NationsBank.

Suddenly, the icon had become ripe for a takedown. Some of the allegations were meaningless tabloid grist: The newsmagazine *Istoe Gente* broke a report of a thirty-two-year-old illegitimate daughter in New York. Unfortunately, he'd left a trail of malfeasance that led to a far more damaging story. Throughout the winter of 2001, the daily *Folha de São Paulo* alleged that Pelé had skimmed $700,000 from a charity match that his company Pelé Sports Marketing had organized for UNICEF, set to be played in Buenos Aires. It was a scheme that involved two shell companies. In response, Pelé pleaded ignorance. He passed blame onto his business partner of twenty years, firing him, then suing him, and dissolving Pelé Sports Marketing. His anger, however, didn't lead him to return the $700,000.

When I asked Pelé's friends about his ethical missteps, they offered several excuses. Some say that Pelé's impoverished upbringing has made him crazy for money.

But they say it's also something a bit more sweet than that, too. When people help him, even unctuous ones, he remains willfully oblivious to their shortcomings. He forgives their mistakes until it's no longer socially acceptable for him to forgive. It's not far from the sociologist Edward Banfield's famous 1958 study of corruption, *The Moral Basis of a Backward Society*. Banfield explained that it's the most familial-based societies, where the sense of obligation is strongest, that breed the worst nepotism and cronyism. In other words, Pelé, and Brazil, weren't just ill-suited for reform. They were ill-suited for capitalism. Pelé could rake in profits. But as much as he told himself that he'd learned to make the cold calculations of the market, he couldn't.

VI.

A few critics ascribe dark motives to the foreign investors. They accuse them of using the clubs to launder money and cover other shady dealings. And, in some cases, there may be truth to this allegation. But most of the foreign investors had arrived in Brazil with a utopian glint in their eyes. All it would take to transform soccer, they theorized, was a bit of transparency, the modern magic of marketing, and exploitation of synergies. They spoke of turning the game into a slick, profitable spectacle—complete with skyboxes and lucrative television contracts. Hicks, Muse of Dallas had even begun the Pan-American Sports Network to televise its teams' games. It was an ambitious plan, and it might have worked had they torn the teams away from *cartolas* like Eurico Miranda.

Miranda invites me to São Januário on the morning after the club's 104th birthday. The night before there had been a gala celebration on the Rio oceanfront. This morning, he's holding a press conference to announce the signing of a highly regarded Serbian émigré named Dejan Petkovic. The celebration the night before, he says, has motivated him "to shake things up." But there's another reason he needs Petkovic. Vasco has had a less than stellar start to the season. By occupying a position near the bottom of the league table, Vasco has threatened Miranda's reelection bid. In the parlance of American political science, the team's poor performance threatens to depress the turnout of Eurico's base. Petkovic is a piece of political pork, a last-minute move to reenergize the club's supporters.

Miranda does little to conceal his ulterior motives. At the press conference, his aides place three burly guys in back of the bank of microphones. Moments before Miranda appears with Petkovic, when the television cameras will turn on, an aide hands the burly men T-shirts with Eurico's name and campaign logo. As journalists enter the press conference, held in the stadium's "presidential conference room," one of Miranda's lackeys offers them a campaign bumper sticker. He screams at a cameraman, "It's not right to wear Bermuda shorts in the office of the president."

In Brazil, Miranda is a familiar figure: the populist. Despite advances toward democracy, his archetype flourishes. These unabashed crooks have no compunction about pocketing money devoted to school lunch programs and steering massive contracts to their family business. But the populists have mastered a few good tricks that make them popular: While they steal for themselves, they also know how to steal for their constituents, pushing money into ostentatious public works projects. It's a style that has been reduced to a common aphorism used to justify support for them, "He steals but he makes."

Miranda enters the press conference. He wears a gold necklace. He has well-oiled hair. One of his long-time critics tells me that about twenty years ago he was a beautiful man. While the beauty may have faded, he still carries himself as if displaying his specimen. Even while Petkovic responds to questions, Miranda demands attention. He sits down in a chair and leans back, proudly exhibiting his corpulence. During the press conference, he smokes a sizeable cigar, rolling it between his fingers as he takes long, hard puffs. It becomes impossible not to stare.

One of the defining characteristics of the Brazilian populist is his pugilism. In a sense, their appeal depends on being perceived as embattled rebels, painting their accusers as uncaring elites. Miranda likes a good fight, too. When Rio's evangelical governor Anthony Garotinho canceled a Vasco match after its stadium disaster, Miranda called him a "weak-kneed" "faggot" "who sat there offering false prayers to Jesus." After a referee sent off three Vasco players in a 1999 game, Miranda stormed onto the field, leading a stampede of his security entourage. Before Miranda could slug the referee, police intervened.

During the Petkovic press conference, Miranda has no compunction about summarily interrupting journalists. "That's a stupid question," he says repeatedly.

Miranda moves a hand in a circular motion, the same one used by a coach to signal a change of players. Fearful perhaps of one of Miranda's verbal rampages, the journalists comply. By the time Miranda finishes his press conference and sits down to talk, I'm a bit fearful too.

I've met many fans of Vasco da Gama, sensible people who disdain corruption but adore Miranda. "He may be a bastard, but he's my bastard" is the classic refrain. Like most strongmen, he can't distinguish between the club's interest and his own—the father figure protecting Vasco from the slings and arrows of a wicked world. He's especially hard on the foreign investors, whom he accuses of trying to destroy his club. "All of a sudden, foreign investors came here and they tried to change this into a thing that they call business. Due to the cultural practices that we have here, they faced several difficulties. Because this approach was not the right one. They came with an objective: Let's take care of the bottom line. Business is that. But that way simply doesn't work here. There are local practices that must be observed. They do know business but they know nothing about our culture, about our local characteristics."

This is highly disingenuous, to say the least. Miranda cut the deal with NationsBank, inviting them into his club. The bank never had anywhere the influence over the club that he alleges. But his use of this rhetoric is incontestably masterful. He's maintained his political base for so long because he's tapped into a powerful line of argument.

Sitting across a conference room table, twirling in his chair, Miranda tells me, "Vasco's a club of immigrants. It was founded by Portuguese and Brazilians.

And Vasco's the only club that has some history. Vasco had the first black player in history. Football was practiced by elites. This is the only club where the associates bought every inch of land with no help from the government. None. It's a pioneer club." Miranda argues that the multinationals will inevitably eviscerate these traditions. The foreign investors will bring in guys "who barely speak Portuguese." In the interest of profit, the foreign investors will try to market the clubs to the widest possible audience. At Palmeiras, the Italian multinational Parmalat changed the team colors. At Corinthians and Flamengo, the foreign investors sold star players to hated cross-town rivals—previously an unthinkable act. Everywhere they went they bragged about their marketing plans. Miranda is trying to argue that foreigners created the impression that clubs are just businesses, not repositories of tradition and superior morality. Miranda's genius was that he only began making these anti-globalization arguments after he robbed the foreign investors blind.

With the departure of foreign investors, Miranda doesn't have any compelling scapegoat that he can flog to distract from his own failings. He campaigns for reelection in the shadow of an atrocious season. Now he doesn't watch games from the honor tribunal, a box at midfield where team presidents traditionally sit. He watches from his own office, which overlooks the pitch, behind dark glass.

Just after visiting with Miranda, I met with an aging ex-Olympic volleyball player named Fernandão. He leads the underground anti-Miranda group, the *Moviemento Unido Vascainos*. It's underground, because

Miranda has thrown Fernandão and his friends out of the club. Today, they buy anti-Miranda billboards near São Januario. They hand out leaflets to Vascainos on their way to watch games at the stadium. Fernandão tells me that the wealth from the NationsBank deal has made Miranda "drunk with power."

A few months later, Fernandão's assessment is borne out. Miranda shows up at the polls with two armed bodyguards. He insists on cutting in front of long lines of voters. Along the way, he pauses to verbally assault a woman reporter. It was too much, even for supporters of Vasco. At the polling place, a revolt begins. Voters start chanting "*ladrão*," thief. By the end of the day, the unthinkable had happened. Miranda had lost, not just his seat in congress, but the parliamentary immunity that came with the seat. The federal prosecutors have been waiting for this day. They have been sitting on a thirty-seven page memo listing Miranda's crimes. After defeating the foreign investors, he is now himself defeated.

With foreign investors out of Brazil, the leading proponent of soccer capitalism became the sports minister, a lifelong technocrat and old friend of President Cardoso called José Luis Portella. He invited me to watch his weekly soccer game, played in a field in northern São Paulo. The players in his league are, by rule, all at least forty-five years old. Portella is a short man, without obvious soccer gifts. He couldn't be further from Pelé, whose old ministry he now occupies. But he's not nearly as physically challenged as some of his teammates. A few are so rotund—diet and fitness have no place in Brazilian masculinity—that they don't ever run for longer than five seconds at a stretch. Several of Portella's teammates are in their mid-sixties. These limitations, however, do little to deter Portella and his teammates from treating the game with the utmost seriousness. The teams have coaches who pace the sidelines cursing their lack of effort and stray passes. They've hired a referee who just retired from administering games in the top Brazilian league. Despite the referee's experience, the players argue with him as much as any group of professionals, if not more. By the end of the first half, the sports minister himself has received a yellow card for screaming in the referee's face.

When Portella and I sit down, he doesn't hide his pessimism about the future of the game. Not even the indictment of Eurico Miranda, he says, would alleviate soccer's deep crisis. But watching Portella play, he undermines his own argument. Even this group of unfit men plays stylishly. They use spin to pass the ball in entirely unexpected directions, shoot with the back of their heals, and showboat their dribbling skills. Despite the persistence of corruption, Brazil's mania for soccer has hardly abated; its natural soccer resources don't seem close to exhausted. It's too essential a part of the national character. As Portella's team scores, the middle-aged men kiss the club's insignia on their jerseys and kiss one another; they tumble into a heap on the field. Even among Brazil's accountants, taxi drivers, and government technocrats, there are moments that make you want to get down on your knees and give thanks to Our Lady of Victories.

6

How Soccer Explains
the Black Carpathians

I.

Edward Anyamkyegh disembarked at Lviv International Airport in the Ukraine precisely ten years into postcommunism. Hints of the old regime could still be detected in the small building. A fading frieze paid tribute to heroic workers carrying their metal tools like swords. Police in brown military hats with large swooping crowns, the kind that used to populate Kremlin Square parades, stared self-importantly at arrivals. Because they were trained to be suspicious of visitors, and because Edward looked so different, the police pulled him aside. *Why have you come to the Ukraine?*

The sight of Edward Anyamkyegh in 2001 may have shocked the police. But in those days, the exhausted end of an era of rapid globalization, his arrival shouldn't have been so disconcerting. It could even be described as one sign of the fading times. In that epoch, strange cultural alchemies had proliferated: Eastern Europeans harvesting Tuscan olive groves; Bengalis answering customer service calls for Delaware credit card companies; and, as in the case of Edward Anyamkyegh, Nigerians playing professional soccer in the Ukraine.

Around the time of Edward's arrival, Nigerians had become a Ukrainian fad. Within a few months, nine Nigerians were signed to play in Ukraine's premier league. They were the most prestigious purchases a club could make. A roster devoid of Nigerians wasn't considered a serious roster; an owner who didn't buy Nigerians wasn't an ambitious owner.

Like all boom markets, the Nigerian fixation betrayed an irrational exuberance. But there was logic behind it, too. During communism, Ukrainian soccer clubs had been state-run enterprises. When the regime ended, however, nobody bothered to privatize them. In many cases, nobody even paid their bills. The situation grew so dire that the Ukrainian game might have disappeared altogether. But the game found its saviors in the country's richest men, the oligarchs. The Ukrainian oligarchs were men who had transitioned seamlessly to capitalism from their slots in the Communist Party bureaucracy, turning insider ties to the old state into new wealth. By covering the expenses, the oligarchs became de facto owners.

The oligarchs announced great ambitions for their new possessions. They told fans that they wanted their teams to take places alongside the greatest clubs of Italy, Spain, and England. To accomplish such a gargantuan task, they would have to imitate the approach of these clubs. One thing in particular caught their attention: the prevalence of black faces. You could see why the Western Europeans had so many of them. Africans had the skills and speed that Ukrainians lacked. They had ingenuity that could make a bland Eastern Bloc team look downright continental.

Lviv had its own oligarch, Petro Dyminskyy. In communism, he'd managed the region's coal mines. After communism, he amassed an incredible fortune—several hundred million dollars reportedly—buying and selling Western Ukraine's bountiful gas, oil, and coal reserves. In the spring of 2001, he added to his holdings the local soccer club, named Karpaty Lviv after the nearby Carpathian mountain range. By investing a small bit of his fortune, Dyminskyy hoped that he could create his own, massively successful team. And with the media glow from this success, he planned on launching a career as a politician, following the Silvio Berlusconi model.

Dyminskyy was no professional soccer man. But he could see the thinking behind the Nigerian purchases made by his fellow owners, and it appealed to him. When an agent from the former Soviet republic of Moldova offered Edward Anyamkyegh for $500,000, Dyminskyy made the purchase. It seemed like a great deal. Everywhere Edward had played, he had scored goals. His c.v. included stints with Nigeria's national under-17 team. He had youth, only twenty-three years, and a muscular upper body that looked suited to the physicality of the Ukrainian game. So when Dyminskyy unveiled his purchase to the people of Lviv, he promised that Edward would help catapult Karpaty to success.

At the time, Dyminskyy showed no signs that he considered this venture to be at all risky. But he had put Edward into Karpaty's green-and-white jersey, covered in Cyrillic lettering, a symbol of Lviv and Ukrainian nationalism. So Edward's arrival at Karpaty represented more than the purchase of a contract, more than a test of a player's mettle and an owner's ability to put together a club. His arrival in the Ukraine was a cross-cultural experiment. In theory, Karpaty's purchase of Edward had followed the rules of globalization to perfection. The Ukrainians had tapped the international labor market and come back with a bargain. To accommodate their new English-speaking purchase, they brought in a new coach who could speak in a language that their new star could understand. Like many companies from the poorer parts of Eastern Europe, they were adhering to the one-world model that had brought great success to thousands of American and European firms. The western strategy of globalization had, in effect, been globalized. But was it suited to the rigors of life and soccer in the Western Ukraine?

II.

Edward walks me to his apartment. It is several blocks deep into one of the old Soviet neighborhoods of endless, relentlessly linear concrete. We met at the neighborhood McDonald's. He brought along his wife and two-year-old girl. His wife, Brecing, has a sincere, soft voice. "You're married? Give a hug to your wife for us. Give her a big kiss," she says, tilting her head. Edward's daughter, wearing cornrows and a jean jacket, stays close to his leg.

For nearly two years, they have lived in this complex. Their daughter was born here. "You see, everyone knows me. We've got no problems. They like me so much." Edward always talks quickly, in a singsong cadence. When he describes his neighbors' affection, he looks to the ground and smirks. As we slowly move toward his home, he points to landmarks. "This is where I play ball with kids . . . this is the bank. You see, bank." He translates the letters from the Cyrillic, one of the few Ukrainian words he says that he can decipher.

The communists didn't build to last; and the post-communists haven't had the resources or desire to repair. Sidewalks and roads have a topography that alternates between piles of pavement and craters. All around, glass facades have shattered. Soot covers the shards that remain in place. Shirts and bags and socks hang from the branches of trees like ornaments.

Although there's nothing too fancy or warm about the interior of the Anyamkyegh apartment, it is an immaculately tended contrast to the dark, dingy hall-way. A tiny oil painting of a flower hangs alone in the living room, with action photos of Edward stuffed into the corner of the frame. In a corner, a mattress lies on the floor with blankets and sheets neatly piled on top. Edward and Brecing sleep here. They like to fall asleep in front of the television. "Sit down," Edward directs me into a chair. He perches on its arm and reaches for the remote. "I have satellite and cable," he says and turns on African American rap music videos.

Edward removes his black Reebok baseball hat, puts his elbow on his knee, and leans on his palm.

"How does a Nigerian find his way to the Ukraine?"

He rubs his hand over his face and begins to nar-rate his journey through the global soccer economy.

For generations, the Anyamkyegh family farmed near the provincial capital of Gboko, not far from Nigeria's eastern border with Cameroon. Edward's father did well by his profession. In a nearby village, he owned groves of mangoes and guava, which he trucked to corners of Nigeria that didn't have such fertile land as Gboko. Returning from his farm one evening, he tried passing a concrete truck in his small car on a narrow highway. Edward was seven when he died.

A decade or two earlier, Edward would have followed his late father into agriculture. Now, there were many distractions. Agents scoured places like Gboko for teens they could sell to European soccer clubs. This sounded glamorous and an opportunity to make unthinkable sums. Boys began to dream of playing on the continent. Enough local examples made these fantasies seem plausible. Queen's Park Rangers of London bought Edward's own older brother, one of seven siblings. And from the time of his father's death, Edward began telling friends that he would become a European star, too.

There was another reason that this wasn't such an implausible notion for Edward: He was a man-child. At fifteen, he had sprouted pectorals and biceps. When the best local professional club bought him, the papers predicted that he would be one of the greatest strikers to ever emerge from Gboko. Word of Edward's talent, how he could outrun the older players and out-muscle the younger ones, reached the coaches of the national squad. They plucked him for a spot on the team sent to the Under-17 World Cup in Ecuador.

A youth team doesn't sound like that big a deal. But in Nigeria, it is an enormous deal. National television broadcasts the team's games. Newspapers closely and harshly monitor its progress. After Edward's team lost to Ghana in the final of the African championship, pundits prodded the coach to purge half his squad. But inevitably it is agents that keep the closest watch. Many of these agents made grandiose promises to Edward. Of the many offers for representation, Edward picked an agent from the Ivory Coast called Ahmed. There was one part of his presentation that Edward liked best: Ahmed said he had already completed a deal with a club in Bordeaux, France.

Just before the World Cup, Edward made his first trip out of Africa. He traveled to the south of France, as wondrous a place as he had imagined. It inspired him to his highest caliber of play. During his two weeks of tryouts, he scored three goals playing on Bordeaux's reserve team. But one afternoon, Edward's agent told him that they would leave France the next day, much earlier than planned. "Why? Why are we going?" Edward asked. "Because there's paperwork that needs to be finished in Africa," his agent replied. Satisfied with the answer, Edward returned to Gboko. Ahmed told him that he would pick him up in a week and they would return together to France. He never came. Later, Edward learned the details of the sordid transaction. Bordeaux had given the agent $5,000 to pay Edward for his tryout. When Bordeaux learned the agent had used this money to bring other Africans to France for auditions with competitor clubs, it scuttled the deal.

This act of venality seemed to curse Edward. Although Nigeria had been a favorite to take the World Cup, the team flamed out in the quarterfinals against minnows from Oman. The result shamed Edward, as did the fact that his teammates had all departed to play for European clubs. The torment of these thoughts prevented Edward from concentrating on the game and maintaining his fitness. Playing for his Gboko club, he ripped thigh muscles in both legs. Because of his state of mind, Edward's Gboko club worried that he would neglect his rehabilitation, ruining any hopes of return. They placed him in a hospital, where he remained for eight months, stuck in his own head.

Edward's return to the pitch has a mythic quality. Inserted in a game—with the coveted Nigerian Challenge Cup on the line, a tied score, and painkillers flowing through him—he added the decisive goal. A few days later, he sat in the back of an open convertible that displayed him to adoring Gboko. A few months later, he achieved his European dream. His new club might not have been nearly as prestigious as Bordeaux. It might not have been even the most prestigious club in the former Soviet Republic of Moldova. But at least the club Sheriff resided in the city of Tiraspol, and Tiraspol was on the continent.

Moldova had experienced its own Nigerian fad. At Sheriff, Edward played with two compatriots. For a season, the arrangement worked wonderfully. Edward scored 11 goals and won player-of-the-month honors. The Moldavians asked Edward to naturalize and play for their national team. But as his eighteen-month contract came to its close, other clubs began to make overtures to him. One team in the United Arab Emirates tendered a lucrative offer that Edward badly wanted to accept. Behind Sheriff's back, he went to visit the prospective team. After Sheriff's ownership expired, he would join them.

Sheriff, however, had other ideas about Edward's fate. It wanted to sell his contract to another club before it expired. That way, they could cash in on Edward's success, too. According to Edward, when club officials learned about his trip abroad, they visited his wife and seized her passport. Edward didn't know how to call the Nigerian embassy and wasn't even sure that a Nigerian embassy existed in Moldova. Upon returning to Moldova, Edward made it clear to the club that he would accept whatever decision they made for him. They decided to sell Edward to Karpaty Lviv.

III.

The Lviv faithful idolize a twenty-eight year-old dentist named Yuri. In addition to expertise in drilling molars and scraping tartar, he captains Karpaty Lviv. As part of the culture of the Soviet game, players often obtained advanced degrees. Besides, only after the arrival of capitalism have players earned salaries that can sustain them through post-playing days. Yuri now earns enough that he doesn't bother practicing. But after he retires, he'll spend a few months reviewing his books and then will open shop in Lviv.

Yuri met me at the Viennese Coffeehouse on Prospekt Svobody, Freedom Avenue. If I didn't know Yuri was local, I could have guessed. Like almost every Ukrainian man in Lviv, he carries a purse and has deep blue eyes. In conversational style, the people of Lviv pride themselves on having an analytical, circumspect manner, an attribute they ascribe to the presence of thirteen universities and thousands of academics in their town. Yuri prefaces every statement with, "I can only speak from my own experience, but. . . ."

Lviv loves Yuri not only for his skills, but because he is one of them. He grew up in Lviv, went to every Karpaty home game as a kid, and wanted nothing more than to play for his beloved team. And they love him, because he represents the city exactly as the people want to see themselves portrayed: articulate, handsome, humble, and hardworking. When he plays badly, he'll admit it without any exculpation. His work rate betrays an inexhaustible passion for his team.

During his captaincy, Yuri has presided over one of the most tumultuous eras in the history of Karpaty. After Edward arrived, the team bought an eighteen-year-old Nigerian attacking midfielder with cornrows, named Samson Godwin. Because the old Ukrainian coach couldn't speak English with the Nigerians, the club brought in a new Serbian manager, who had spent ten years playing for Southampton Football Club in England. The Serb, in turn, recruited four players from former Yugoslav countries. Suddenly, Yuri skippered a polyglot unit that included a coach and players whose languages he couldn't himself speak.

This was a big change for Karpaty. Even in the Soviet era, it had been renowned for its localism. Where most Ukrainian clubs contained players from Russia and the other republics, Karpaty consisted almost exclusively of men from Lviv and its environs.

This meant that Karpaty games reflected the implicit political reality of Western Ukraine: Lviv viewed itself as struggling against Russian masters who had imposed communism upon them. Of course, it was dangerous to make anything of Karpaty's political symbolism. The state was always listening. An old-time chairman of the club has admitted that he supplied the KGB with Karpaty tickets, so agents could overhear any politically tinged shouts in the stadium. Nevertheless, people deeply felt the connection between their club and their national aspirations. When Karpaty won the USSR Cup in 1969, its fans sang Ukrainian songs in the Moscow stadium. The people of Lviv watching the game at home on television wept at the sound of their language resounding through the capital of their conquerors.

As he drank tea, Yuri explained this history. "Karpaty never had political power; it never will have more money than the clubs in Kiev or Donetsk [the industrial capital of Eastern Ukraine]. But it has had a sense of spirit that has helped make up for these disadvantages. The big moments in Karpaty's history happened when the team had local players and unity."

With the arrival of the foreigners, the team had nothing resembling unity. It broke down into factions. You would walk into the team dining room and find the various nationalities eating at their own separate tables. They would sit apart on the team bus and at practice. For sure, it didn't help matters that the Ukrainians couldn't converse with the Nigerians. (They had a much easier time integrating the Yugoslavs, whose language has close relations with Ukrainian and whose culture has the same Slavic underpinnings.) There were, however, less appealing reasons for this split within the team. Edward had been the most expensive acquisition in the history of the club. He earned, his teammates imagined, much more than they did.

Yuri had become particularly perturbed with the Nigerians. Too many of his fellow Ukrainians complained that the Nigerians weren't trying very hard. Yuri agreed with this assessment. He felt the Nigerians didn't run enough or sacrifice their bodies. The Karpaty jersey didn't mean anything to them. For goodness sake, Edward and Samson said quite freely that they viewed the Ukraine as a mere way station on their routes toward the leagues of Western Europe. He felt their arrogance and indifference would tear the club apart.

After one practice, Yuri pulled Edward and Samson aside. He told them that they needed to increase their effort, to work with the rest of the team. "They were somehow offended with such a conversation," he recounted to me. The next thing he knew, "Edward and Sampson went to Dyminskyy [the president of the club] and told him that players weren't giving passes to the Nigerians. The president met with me. He was furious, 'Why isn't the team giving passes to the Nigerians?' I told him, 'Do you not think I'm giving my best? I live for this team.'"

A day after meeting Yuri, I watched Karpaty practice. They trained in a village meadow. A rusty old rail car stood at one end of the field, a place for players to change clothes, although most players preferred to strip in public view. Team owner Petro Dyminskyy sat under an awning in front of this car. Even though it was a hot spring day, he wore black. He remained ominously silent through the proceedings. The team went through its drills—small groups playing games of keep away, exercises in crossing and heading the ball. For each of these, Edward and Samson worked together. None of the other players volunteered to join them. Coaches filled those vacancies, even the Serbian head coach joined to give enough bodies. Under the blazing May sun, they worked their well-fed middle-aged bodies into supersaturated sponges of sweat.

IV.

On a street corner outside my hotel, I tried to make conversation with two sportswriters. One had been trained as an atomic scientist. Neither really spoke much English. We waited for a translator to arrive. As they filled the awkward silences with the phrases they knew, Edward serendipitously drove past us in an old beat-up cab with a cracked windshield. His driver slowed down for a moment and he put his hand out the window. I grabbed it. The other writers nodded in his direction. When Edward turned the corner, one of them chuckled. "Monkey," he said in English. "Bananas," the other one chimed.

It is difficult to gauge how much of the resentment toward the Nigerians should be described as racism. Clearly, many of the Ukrainian players feel the same as the journalists. They would complain to team officials that "they didn't want to play with monkeys." The Serbian coach told me, "I was surprised that some of the young kids on the team don't like black kids. This is not the way we should think in Europe. You associate Europe with civilization. That's typical thinking for primitive people. You can feel how isolated [the Ukrainians] were in lots of manners and their way of thinking and so on."

Yet their hatred doesn't betray isolation, but the opposite. There's a strange uniformity in the vocabulary European soccer fans use to hate black people. The same primate insults get hurled. Although they've gotten better over time, the English and Italians developed the tradition of making ape noises when black players touched the ball. The Poles toss bananas on the field. This consistency owes nothing to television, which rarely shows these finer points of fan behavior. Nor are these insults considered polite to discuss in public. This trope has simply become a continent-wide folk tradition, transmitted via the stadium, from fan to fan, from father to son.

Based on its history, you might imagine racism to be the logical conclusion of Lviv's historical trajectory away from pluralism. Once upon a time, Lviv truly exuded cosmopolitanism. It was the kind of place you might expect to find odd cultural alchemies. When the Austro-Hungarian Empire ruled, until World War I, the town was filled with grand opera houses and ornate coffee houses, like the one where Yuri and I took tea. It acquired the frilly atmospherics of *Mitteleuropa*. An energetic mix of ethnicities—Poles, Jews, Germans, Russians, and Ukrainians—helped give substance to this worldly aesthetic. The Lviv melting pot brewed schools of philosophy, great universities, poets, and world-class intellectuals, like the economist Ludwig Van Mises and the ethicist Martin Buber.

Considering that Lviv had been founded as a Ukrainian fortress, many Ukrainians found it strange that their people had achieved so little in the city's era of greatness. They began to harbor deep resentments toward the presence of so many interlopers. During World War II, they seized opportunities to clean up this mess. Many local Ukrainians worked with the Germans to eliminate the Jews—who once accounted for about 30 percent of Lviv's populace. Then, following the war, in a move sanctioned by Stalin, they deported the Polish half of town en masse. Finally, with the Poles and Jews purged, the Ukrainians could leave their villages and take up residence in Lviv's vacant houses.

Upon arriving in Lviv, the Ukrainians compensated for years of self-pity by developing a new theory of their own superiority. They looked east toward the other big Ukrainian cities—Kiev, Odessa, Donetsk—and saw Russians mixing with Ukrainians. Without a fight, the easterners had exchanged the Ukrainian language for Russian, intermarried, and embraced the Soviet system. Quietly, in their homes, so as not to draw the attention of the Communist apparatus, they dismissed these other Ukrainians as cultural traitors.

In the atmosphere of nationalism and resentment, however, racism doesn't really exist. Aside from the odd, crude paroxysm of hate, the situation isn't nearly as nasty as in the West. At games, fans don't make ape noises when Edward enters the field or touches the ball. Even the racism of players can't compare to the leagues in England and Italy. In the Karpaty locker room, the

Ukrainians never have overtly racial confrontations with the Nigerians.

The difference is this: Lviv has 830,000 residents and only fifty Africans. Except for Edward and Samson, most of them study at Lviv's universities and will leave the Ukraine in a few years. There are simply not enough to generate friction or a political backlash or ideology. No fringe groups like the British National Party or politicians like France's Jean-Marie Le Pen stoke and politicize the hatred. Ukrainian feelings are too primitive to even warrant the suffix "ism." They feel something closer to a naïf's dislike of the unfamiliar, like an eight-year-old refusing to try dinner at an Ethiopian restaurant.

Trailing Edward through Lviv, this reaction becomes plain. Sitting with him at McDonald's, I looked up and noticed a little blond girl with a yellow duck on her red shirt, staring slack-jawed at Edward. When she pointed out Edward to her brother, he entered the very same state of shock. They covered their mouths to contain their laughter. Their mother tried to turn them away, embarrassed by the rudeness. But she kept casting looks at Edward, too. When I pointed them out to Edward, he told me that they probably hadn't seen a black man outside of the television set in their living room. "No problem."

There's another reason for the hostility toward the Nigerians at Karpaty. It has to do with the politics of postcommunism. After the Soviet Union collapsed, Ukrainians began the project of cultural and national regeneration. You could see the push in their two most beloved institutions, their language and church. The remaining Jews and Russians of Lviv who didn't speak Ukrainian were bullied and shamed into switching vernaculars. Across the city, old Ukrainian churches were reclaimed from Soviet ruin. The postcommunist government restored the Museum of Atheism to its baroque greatness. Crosses went back into these buildings. In fact, crosses began appearing everywhere, on hilltops and in the squares. Celebrations of Easter, once prohibited, became cause for grand investment in traditional costumes and meals.

When Edward arrived, the national ego was particularly fragile. Ten years into postcommunism the joys of freedom had begun to feel commonplace; the project of Ukrainian regeneration seemed stalled. To many Ukrainians, their country still felt like a colony of Russia. Those who spoke of an alternative to this condition didn't have a much more appealing solution. They proposed that the Ukraine become (more or less) a client state of the European Union and the United States.

This despair played out in soccer, too. Ukrainians imagined that they once were a great soccer nation. Now they needed to import Nigerians to become great again. This fact couldn't be read any other way: It was a humiliation. It was short-term thinking of the worst kind. If the oligarchs wanted the Ukraine to become a great soccer nation again, why not invest the money spent on Edward into the development of young Ukrainian talent? Yuri, the captain, told me, "For the price of Edward we could have created ten Ukrainian players."

V.

Edward doesn't like to admit that he has enemies or problems. In part, he is an affable guy. At practice, only Edward entertained the neighborhood kids hanging around their heroes. He recruited one to assist in his practice of headers. When he finished, he walked over to muss his little helper's hair. But Edward also tries to bite his tongue, so that he doesn't earn any ill will that could ultimately interfere with his dream of playing in Western Europe. I first became aware of his whitewashing on a visit to his apartment. He showed me photos that he'd just developed. A few of the snapshots documented team training sessions in February. I asked him if it was hard to play in the Ukrainian winter. "No problem. It's not so bad," he said.

His answer flew in the face of everything I'd heard about Ukrainian winters—precisely what you'd expect of the Carpathian foothills. Conditions become so arctic that the league takes nearly four months off in the middle of the season. It is simply too cruel to play every week. When the club returned from its last winter break, an army unit spent seven days breaking through fifteen-centimeter-thick ice that crusted the stadium. The restart of the season in early March, however, hardly coincides with the spring thaw. Last year, Karpaty played a game with the thermometer stuck at minus 30 degrees centigrade, and even this reading doesn't actually represent a significant deviation from the norm.

In Edward's photos, the club trains on a snow-covered surface. Sand demarcates the sidelines. Even the ruddy Ukrainians line up in wool hats, long pants, and heavy parkas. Many Nigerians playing in the Ukraine complain bitterly about their inability to maneuver in these temperatures. They say that their frozen feet feel like sledgehammers, while their style of play demands a chisel's delicacy. Ukrainian sportswriters have pointed out that the Nigerians tend to score all their goals in the early autumn and late spring. Looking at Edward in the photo, with his arms pulled close to his trunk, it becomes perfectly evident that the Ukrainian winter is very much a problem for him, too.

Weather may be the biggest shock for Nigerians. But it isn't the only one. Ukrainian soccer culture clashes violently with the style of play to which Nigerians are accustomed. More than almost any other country in the world, the Ukrainians have an idiosyncratic approach to the game. The man behind the approach was a coach, trained as a plumber, called Valeri Lobanovsky. Applying the logic of scientific Marxism to the game, he believed that soccer could be mastered by uncovering the game's mathematical underpinnings. He created a system of numerical values to signify every "action" in a game. As he envisioned it, a group of "scientists" would tally passes, tackles, and shots. These scientists would note "successful actions" and "unsuccessful actions." Their data would be run through a computer, which would spit back an evaluation of the player's "intensitivity," "activity," "error rate," and "effectivity."

Lobanovsky intermittenly coached the club Dynamo Kiev for decades and later headed the Ukrainian national team. His system became gospel, internalized by generations of coaches and players. Even after his death in 2002, the national federation continues to send scientists to every single Ukrainian professional game. His system rewards a very specific style of play: physical and frenetic. Players work tirelessly to compile points. They play defense more aggressively than offense, because that's where points can be racked up. In a way, Lobanovsky's system mimicked the Soviet regime under which it was conceived. Like the Soviets, it stifles individual initiative. Nothing in Lobanovsky's point valuation measures creativity or daring. A vertical pass receives the same grade as a horizontal pass; a spectacular fake means nothing.

Compounding the stultifying effect of Lobanovsky, Ukrainians have made a fetish of coaching. Managers play a role akin to the Communist Party, imposing rigid strategic formations and an authoritarian culture. Ukrainian players commonly glance at their coach, trying to glean whether they have won his approval. Human agency has no place in this world.

The Ukrainian game couldn't be more different from the Nigerian one. The paradigm ruling Nigerian soccer treats the game less as science than art. Nigeria is the Brazil of Africa—clever, undisciplined, and stylish. Ukrainians maniacally fling themselves at the ball, no matter its location on the field; Nigerians are trained to conserve energy and chase the ball more selectively. In addition, they attack differently. Ukrainians like to score goals by quickly exploiting lapses in the defense, moving the ball across the field with long passes. They often execute predetermined plays, with players moving in predetermined patterns, plays as intricate as any conceived by Vince Lombardi. Nigerians, on the other hand, are used to a more deliberate pace of offense, where skills and short passes create opportunities.

All this is a way of excusing Edward's sub par performance for Karpaty—and the failure of the other Africans in the Ukraine to achieve their potential. In two years, Edward has barely scored. Despite his abundance of natural gifts, Edward never looks natural on the Ukrainian field. Players bang into him as he shoots, something he'd never experienced before. Coaches and teammates demand that he play defense. Because he never learned the art of tackling, he's always mistiming his slides and accumulating ridiculous fouls.

When I attended a Karpaty game, the club desperately needed to win. The season would only stretch for two more months, and only a narrow sliver buffered them from the relegation zone. At this defining juncture, the coach pulled Edward from the starting lineup for the first time in his stay with Karpaty. The coach played him less than five minutes as a substitute in the game's finale. Edward ran hard up and down the right wing. But only once in this spell did the ball touch his foot.

After the game, we met outside the locker room. Every other player seemed elated—or at least relieved— by the outcome of the game, a one-nothing win.

"Congratulations," I told Edward.

"Why congratulate me? I played five minutes. I did nothing."

This dismissive tone and naked insecurity seemed totally out of character. Even if Edward's mannerisms and tone of voice often betrayed nerves, his words always conveyed complete confidence. After his contract expired, he said he would move to a league in Western Europe. "Spain is a place I'd like to go next." But outside the locker room, he faced the frightening fact that his career in the Ukraine might not last much longer.

Edward's teammates had already changed out of their uniforms and boarded the team bus that would drop them in downtown Lviv. A throng of jubilant Karpaty fans had sent them off. Edward didn't join his comrades. An official from the Ukrainian federation had picked Edward for a random drug test, and the coaching staff wanted to put Edward on the scale. They were concerned that excess pounds had slowed him down. Edward walked around the Karpaty facility in bare feet, still wearing his kit.

"I don't understand why the coach and the general director want to weigh me. They don't weigh anyone else. No other players. They say I'm too heavy. But I was 77 kilos when I came here." He gently grabbed my elbow to make sure that I paid attention. "Now, I'm 71. I don't know why they have a problem with me. Why do they have a problem with me?"

The groundskeeper interrupted Edward. He wanted to lock up the stadium. With his hand, he made a gesture to Edward to stop talking, to gather his clothes, and leave.

"You see, I am man of the world," the Serb coach Ivan Golac says. In an accent that contains only slight traces of his Balkan roots, he ticks off evidence supporting this claim. He keeps his main residence in Vienna. During the summer, he decamps to an apartment in France, just over the border from Spain, where he walks quiet mountain paths with his wife. But more than being a man of the world, he is, at heart, a man of England.

Golac's case of Anglophilia began as a teenage obsession. Before even the arrival of such a term in communist Belgrade, he was a flower child. He wore his hair shoulder-length and acquired a fanatical interest in the English music scene that went far deeper than the Stones, the Kinks, and The Who. Swinging London had a soccer outpost, the World Cup–winning English team of the sixties. They played with such enthusiasm and panache that Golac desperately wanted to join them. "I dreamed only of playing in England." For a decade, he lived his dream, playing in Southampton and living like a country squire in verdant southern England.

Like Edward, Golac has been flung far and wide by the soccer economy. When the opportunity at Karpaty opened, a stint coaching with an Icelandic outfit across the bay from Reykjavik had just ended. "A friend told me there was a club in the Ukraine with an ambitious owner. This interested me greatly." By the time we sat down in the Viennese Coffeehouse and ordered ice cream, he had survived four months of Ukrainian soccer. The beginning of his tenure had not gone well. Golac arrived at Karpaty and immediately ushered in an era of losing. His English understanding of the game didn't jibe with the habits of the Lobanovsky-steeped players. Team officials would gasp at his predilection for empowering players to make tactical decisions on the fly. And players would look like soccer idiots when handed a little piece of on-field volition. "It was a shock to me. They were not allowed to think." The Nigerian problem needed to be dealt with, too. Nobody could deny that the team chemistry experiment had created corrosive compounds.

When I first met Golac, he made it clear that he considered himself blessed to have avoided Serbia in wartime. The hacking apart of multi-ethnic Yugoslavia saddened and disgusted him. In his condemnation of Ukrainian racism, he invoked this position again. "I know nationalism and was surprised at how strong it is here."

"They're good boys," he said, turning the subject to Edward and Samson. "It's hard for the African players to adapt, especially when you have training sessions at minus 25. It's hard enough for us continental people. I can't imagine for them. They get very low, very depressed. That's where you've got to be very careful, very gentle with them."

Listening to him talk in his confident pianissimo voice, I imagined him to be a superb psychologist. In training, I noticed that he effectively criticized players without jabbing their egos. I pressed him to explain to his methodology. "Describe the gentle approach?"

"I've told them, 'You've got ability, boys. You've got ambition, I suppose. If you don't do well, if you're not disciplined, if you're not ambitious enough, and can't match my ambition, I'll send you back to Africa.' "

Our conversation put me in the mind of the previous week. After presiding over a string of bitter losses, the coach had decided to call on God for help. The team visited a village church, not far from Karpaty's training complex, fifteen minutes from Lviv's city center.

On the Christian family tree, Ukrainians have their own divergent branch called Greek Catholicism. As church architecture evinces, the denomination shares many of Russian Orthodoxy's traits and traditions. This small village church has a cupola with a Red Square–like cap of silver that tapers around a distinctly eastern curve. Inside, icons of the medieval, pre-perspective style abound. They are displayed in a three-tiered gold-leaf altarpiece.

As the team bus made its way to the church, it passed a family in a horse-drawn cart and peasant women using shovels to dig rows in front-yard plots. When Karpaty arrived at church, the last service hadn't yet finished. The team piled out of the bus and bided time on the rocky road in front of the church. As always, Edward and Samson stood together. In their tracksuits and sneakers, they hardly looked prepared for the sacred.

Across the road, the coaches and trainers waited in their own group. The club's chief assistant coach, a hard-looking man with a martial flattop, entertained them. "Edward is always crossing himself." He bowed his head and made the Greek Catholic gesture with vaudevillian exaggeration. The management laughed. "I wish the Ukrainian boys did the same more often." He clasped his hands, looked toward the sky, and sarcastically smiled. The management laughed some more.

After a few minutes of awkwardly waiting, the club's executive director signaled that Karpaty should file into the church. The Ukrainians traced crosses on their chests in rapid succession at almost every door jam and juncture; their hands never falling to their sides. In an entryway, they stopped to kiss the feet of a crucifix hung on an almost-hidden sidewall. A thickly bearded priest in billowing white robes chanted the end of the liturgy.

While the Ukrainians enthusiastically moved toward the priest, Karpaty's two Muslim players, both from the ex-Yugoslavia, stopped near the back of the church. Although they seemed to concentrate hard on the ritual, they shifted their hands from their pockets to behind their backs and into their pockets again. The Ukrainians—and the Greek Catholic church—had robustly backed their Slavic Serb brothers in their war against Bosnia's Muslims. When the priest's scepter lobbed holy water over Karpaty, the two players took matador steps to the side.

Without a word of explanation, the priest then disappeared behind the altar and resumed chanting. One by one, players moved toward the front of the church and performed the Greek Catholic rituals. Edward tried to imitate the Ukrainians: a cross of the chest; a kneel to the ground, a kiss on an icon of Jesus in his death shroud; a wiping away of lip marks with cloth; the cycle repeated.

Edward rose. Following his teammates, he walked to the gold altar. In front of the icons, he went down to his knees. He crossed himself, folded his hands, closed his eyes, and prayed.

7

How Soccer Explains the New Oligarchs

I.

Pierluigi Collina's fame defies all the laws of sporting celebrity. His haunted-house looks include a Kojak pate, tubercular gauntness, and Beetlejuice eyes springing forth from their sockets. He runs like an ostrich. There is, however, something far stranger about his celebrity: He is not a player but a referee.

To be fair, he isn't just any bureaucratic enforcer of the rulebook. Collina is roundly considered the premier practitioner of his trade. He has presided—with a combination of exceptional hardheadedness and sensitive diplomacy—over World Cup finals and heated rivalries like the Falkland War rematches between England and Argentina. His renown is now such that he appears in Adidas ads alongside David Beckham, Zinedine Zidane, and other virtuosos. *GQ* fashion spreads, and countless magazine profiles, capture him in his manicured villa, playing lovingly with his pet dogs.

Not just in America, but in any country, this adoration would seem strange. But Italians have endowed their referees with celebrity. Collina's colleagues have stood for parliament and retired into comfy careers as television commentators. Referees have achieved this notoriety, because Italian media devotes so much careful attention to every yellow card disbursed and every sweeping tackle ignored. Newspapers use star rating systems to judge their work, as with restaurants or movies. They regularly publish statistical analyses— down to the second decimal point—that try to uncover the true biases of referees. A highly watched television program called *Il Processo,* the trial, sits a jury of journalists and retired players that vivisects the minutiae of controversial calls. In refereeing the referees, the jurors rely on an array of technological tools. Super slow motion can show a player onside by sixteen centimeters. Like a Cindy Sherman art film, *Il Processo* endlessly repeats footage of falling players, so that the jury can precisely determine if he faked his plummet.

To understand the importance of refereeing requires a brief word on the paradox of Italian soccer. As everyone knows, Italian men are the most foppish representatives of their sex on the planet. They smear on substantial quantities of hair care products and expend considerable mental energies color-coordinating socks with belts. Because of their dandyism, the world has Vespa, Prada, and Renzo Piano. With such theological devotion to aesthetic pleasure, it is truly perplexing that their national style of soccer should be so devoid of this quality.

Starting in the 1960s, the Italians began practicing a highly defensive strategy called *catenaccio,* the lock-down. This formation adds an extra layer of defense, a sweeper, bringing up the rear of an already robust back line that marks man-to-man. Offense doesn't usually receive many resources in this arrangement. Goals are scored in bursts of counterattack, with the ball quickly sent up the field in flashes. This way, goals come with great rarity, usually only once or twice a game. With so few opportunities to score, and so little margin of error, players must do whatever they can to gain the upper hand. Thus, the greatest cliché of Italian soccer—the impassioned two-handed *mamma mia* pleading with the referee.

Even as the old *catenaccio* style has been heavily modified in recent years to provide more offense, the tropes of the system remain. Complaints and games-manship are still meant to provide the decisive advan-tage in games. Players flop in hopes of deceiving the referee into awarding a penalty. They argue the justice of every decision, calculating that they can plant enough doubt to earn a make-up call later in the game. After every goal, defenders hold up their arms in protest, as if this gesture might pry up a linesman's offside flag.

Because of the referee's centrality to the outcome of games, teams do whatever they can to influence him. Almost every year, there's a new debate over the proce-dure for assigning referees. Under the current system, a two-person committee winnows down the pool of ref-erees before their names go into a random draw. One member of the committee is known to be backed by the most powerful clubs, Juventus of Turin and AC Milan. The other represents the rest of the league. The result is that Juve and Milan often can rig the system to assign themselves the most mediocre, provincially minded referees, who are (subconsciously) more deferential toward their prestige clubs. The famed Collina and similarly scrupulous colleagues are rarely ever sent to preside over Juve matches. Other referees who have issued critical penalties against Juve have found themselves working games in the lowly Serie B.

This is only the overt rigging that we know about. Clearly, much more goes on behind the scenes. The fact that Milan and Juventus have so much power over the selection process is itself damning evidence of funny business, begging a long series of questions about the transactions between club chairmen in smoky rooms. Everyone testifies to these sub rosa shenanigans but they rarely have concrete evidence to prove it. On only a few occasions have some of the submerged sordid details come to surface. In 1999, the daily sports paper *Gazzetta dello Sport* exposed that the club AS Roma had given each of Italy's top referees a $13,500 Rolex—an event dubbed "Night of the Watches." Not one of the referees, the report revealed, had voluntarily returned the gift.

Undeniably, the benefits of friendly refereeing accrue to Juventus and Milan more than any other clubs in Italy. And in a way, that's not shocking. Big, historically dominant teams universally seem to get the benefit of the doubt. But Italian manipulation of referees is a far more deliberate affair. Juventus and Milan take two very different paths to winning generous treatment, and these two different modes don't just reveal contrasting organizations. They reveal critical differences between their owners—the most powerful forces in postwar Italy and representatives of two very different styles of oligarchy.

Juve is a toy of the Agnelli family, owners of Fiat and of a substantial percentage of the Milan stock exchange. As much as anyone in Europe, the Agnellis represent the preglobalization style of ruling class that dominated much of the Latin world for the twentieth century. Even though the Agnellis are industrialists, at the height of their powers they behaved like the landowning families that ruled Central America. They did little to advertise their influence, preferring to hide behind the curtains, while they quietly controlled the politicians who regulated their business empires. Their shyness contributed to a longstanding problem in Italian politics: Nobody could locate the true centers of power, a condition that exacerbated the longstanding Italian penchant for worrying about conspiracies. Despite the system's obtuseness, it has become clear that it worked like this: a coalition of northern industrialists, corrupt Christian Democratic politicians, and the southern Mafia ran the country. Politicians lived off bribes from industrialists, and the industrialists survived on the state contracts they received in return. Only with the "clean hands" anti-corruption investigations of the early nineties, and the indictment of hundreds of politicians, did this system topple.

For most of the postwar era, Juventus has had the same sort of dominance as the Agnellis, broken only for a short spell in the sixties. It became a kind of

national squad for Italians, with more followers scattered across the peninsula than any other team. But in
the eighties, Juve found its stranglehold seriously challenged by AC Milan. The arrivistes owed their new success almost entirely to their flamboyant owner, Silvio
Berlusconi. Within the course of two decades, he built
his own massive empire, starting with real estate, extending to television, newspapers, advertising, and insurance. Eight years after buying the club in 1986, he rode
its success to the pinnacle of power, the Italian premier-
ship, an office he now occupies for the second time.

According to Berlusconi's critics on the left, his tan-
gle of interests represents a danger to democracy, the
harbinger of the new dictator: the Citizen Kane media
mogul who can manipulate and control public discourse to ensure such profits and power that he will
never be effectively challenged. And in the globalized
economy, they argue, the media has so much more
power. No longer do these moguls really have to compete with state-owned television networks, or fight for
market share against state companies, which have
been enfeebled by privatization and deregulation. Now
that moguls like Silvio Berlusconi can operate on a
global stage, they can develop economies of scale that
make them even more oligarchic and politically
untouchable.

But there are key differences that separate the new
oligarchs from their forerunners. Because they trade
shares of their companies on stock markets and cut
deals with multinational corporations, the current
breed of mogul has a harder time obscuring wealth and
influence. And even if they could, such humility would

play counter to type. Like Berlusconi, they are new money inclined to flaunt their riches. Consequently, everyone knows and understands their conflicts of interest. Of course, this doesn't excuse the sins of the new moguls—and it certainly doesn't excuse Berlusconi's bribes, manipulation of government to promote his own interests, and other alleged criminalities—but it makes them more transparent, and in an odd way a democratic advance over the old regimes.

II.

When Berlusconi bought Milan, it was a team with a glorious past that had stumbled onto hard times. He made it great again, by infusing it with flash, foreign players, and his nose for spectacle. Juventus has an entirely different style. They have always been great and exuded the understatement of old money. Its owners, the Agnellis, are often referred to as the "unofficial Italian monarchy." Where Berlusconi tries to cast a populist persona, the Agnellis prefer a patrician one. The cravat-wearing, late paterfamilias Gianni Agnelli was the dashing European playboy par excellence. He cavorted with Jackie Kennedy and Rita Hayworth. He spent years tuning out Italy's postwar devastation, lounging on the Riviera.

Because the Agnellis didn't advertise their wealth and power, it is easy to underestimate them. By one count, in the early nineties, the Agnellis influenced or controlled banking, insurance, chemicals, textiles, armaments, financial services, cement, and publishing businesses with a total market worth of about $60 billion. That's roughly a third of the entire capitalization of the Milan stock exchange. Fiat controlled a substantial share of the Rizzoli publishing empire and important papers, including the *Corriere della Sera,* the *New York Times* of Italy. It would be odd if this much money and influence didn't buy enormous power. According to an old joke, the role of the Italian prime minister is to polish the Agnellis' doorknob. They considered it their right to exert influence on policy. "Industrialists are ministerial by definition," Gianni Agnelli's grandfather once proclaimed.

Juventus have the nickname Old Lady, an unlikely appellation for a club run by so stylish an owner as Gianni Agnelli. Despite flashy foreign stars and occasional periods of entertaining play, their style has often been an extension of their drab black-and-white uniforms. Their defensiveness and tactical obsessions leave little margin for error and much in the hands of referees. Nevertheless, Juventus sit as the unofficial monarchy of Italian soccer. Since 1930, when the professional game began, Juventus have won twenty-five championships and finished second fourteen times.

What's shocking about this record, aside from the sheer dominance it represents, is how often Juventus have won the championship at the end of the season on a piece of dubious refereeing. Footage of these officiating travesties can be viewed on the Web site www.anti-Juve.com. It is worth seeing with one's own eyes the phantom penalties that have deprived Juve's opponents of vital goals. You'll see clips of the ball crossing Juve's goal line, yet inexplicably not counted against them.

A recent example from this history of infamy perfectly illustrates the critics' case. In 1998, Juve won the so-called "season of poison." They triumphed because referees denied Juve's opponents clear goals and failed to properly punish Juve's sins. Even though Juve committed more fouls than any club in the league, they received the least red cards, a statistical inconsistency that defies logical reckoning. The season came to be summarized by a match against their closest rivals, Inter Milan. After a Juve player blatantly body-checked Inter's Brazilian striker Ronaldo, the referee declined to award Inter a penalty. A bit later, on the other side of the field, he granted Juve a dubious penalty for a transparent piece of thespianism, where the cause of a player's flop to the ground could not be explained by any known law of physics. The whole game was so pathetically adjudicated that even an Angelli-owned paper, *La Stampa,* condemned the handing of the championship trophy to Juventus. "One cannot remain indifferent when confronted with certain coincidences that are so singular, and, let's say 'nutritious.'..."

After that season, Juventus's strength became, once again, the subject of intense public debate. In a parliamentary session, a postfascist politician called Domenico Gramazio railed against the pro-Juve travesties. "A lot of Italian referees drive Fiats," he exclaimed loudly in the well of the Italian legislature. His accusations deeply wounded one of his colleagues, a former Juventus player named Massimo Mauro. In response to the attacks on his club's honor, Mauro began chanting "Clown, clown." It took gold-braided ushers to prevent Gramazio from punching Mauro. To prevent further escalation and further humiliation, the deputy prime minister abruptly closed the session.

Gramazio went a step further than the evidence. Aside from isolated cases in the distant past, there's no direct evidence linking Juventus to enormous bribes. Nevertheless, the Juventus record looks too suspicious to be chalked up to mere serendipity and stray referee error. Besides, we know too much about the style of Agnelli, Fiat, and Italy's postwar oligarchy. There's no doubt that Agnelli built Fiat into an industrial giant by dint of superb, charismatic management. And there's no doubt that his management tactics included bribing politicians. He has admitted as much. In the early nineties, Agnelli confessed that Fiat had paid $35 million worth of bribes over the course of the previous ten years. Although Fiat had more power than most corporations, it was hardly alone in slipping stuffed envelopes beneath the table. Under the monopolistic rule of the Christian Democratic Party—an organization that formed the bedrock of every postwar Italian government until the 1990s—bribery was a regularized feature of Italian business. Politicians would sign government contracts with the corporations and install high tariffs to protect them. In return, the corporations helped consolidate the Christian Democrats' control and slipped the politicians a big tip for their help. Carlo De Benedetti, the magnate who ran the industrial giant Olivetti, described postwar Italy as "closer to the Arab souk than to Brussels."

But after the "clean hands" investigations of the early nineties, this system broke down. Agnelli's right-hand man found himself indicted on all sorts of corruption charges. Deprived of political patrons and forced to compete in a liberalized European market, Fiat was pummeled by foreign competitors and began wallowing in debt. It began shedding its non-automobile businesses, focusing its energies on salvaging its core from fatal decay.

Here the analogy between politics and sport breaks down. The events of the 1990s had no parallel in soccer. Juventus's prestige and dominance have hardly suffered. But now they have a formidable competitor for dominance in the new oligarch Silvio Berlusconi's AC Milan.

III.

The Italian intelligentsia paints an ominous portrait of Silvio Berlusconi. To launch his early real estate projects, they assert, he indentured himself to the Mafia for seed money. Berlusconi only ran for political office, they allege, after his political patron fled to Tunisia to evade jail, leaving his corrupt businesses exposed. When the journalists he employs challenge him, he often squashes their careers.

With this damning image in mind, it wasn't a promising development when AC Milan kidnapped me. The event transpired two days after the club won its sixth Champions League title—a pedestal that only Real Madrid had ever reached. That morning in my hotel room, I called Milan's communications director, a jovial fellow called Vittorio. Like almost everyone in the organization, he is a Berlusconi man. He goes back years with Fininvest, the holding company that contains the whole of the Berlusconi empire, starting as a reporter for an entertainment digest, then winding his way through the AC Milan bureaucracy.

"Take a taxi and be here in fifteen minutes, okay?" He gave me an address on one of Milan's fanciest streets. I had other appointments scheduled that day, but couldn't refuse his help.

When I arrived, a bearded man in a leather jacket shook my hand firmly. "Frank? Excuse me. One moment, please." He picked up his cell phone, turned his back to me, and began talking quickly but softly. A German car pulled up beside us. "Let's go," he said, prying the bottom of the phone from his face. I had anticipated that we would have a coffee or sit down in his office. Now in a car racing through Milan with typical Italian velocity, I was unsure of our destination. On the phone, he hadn't mentioned anything about any trips, certainly not any involving the many kilometers of autostrada we were now crossing.

Finally, Vittorio returned the phone to his pocket. Because I was too embarrassed by my ignorance of our destination, I didn't ask the obvious, clarifying questions. But soon, Vittorio had told me enough that I realized we were going to Milan's training grounds, a facility that goes by the name Milanello.

"When will we be going back to the city? I have appointments this afternoon," I asked.

"Who knows?" He turned around in the front seat and smiled broadly. "Don't worry. The AC Milan press office will take very good care of you." Vittorio slapped my knee.

AC Milan likes to cultivate an image of glamour. Milanello, even in its lush-sounding name, exudes it in spades. With the low-slung buildings surrounded by trellised terraces, a rose garden, and beautifully land-scaped groves, it wouldn't have surprised me if Milanello had belonged to a viscount with a sizeable trust fund.

"You will take a stroll around," Vittorio announced, placing a hand on my back. "But first lunch." After ordering me an espresso at the team bar, he guided me into an executive dining room where teenage play-ers were taking leisurely lunches in high-backed mod-ern chairs.

The entire building had been impeccably decorated. Doors are painted a lacquered red with black trim, the team's colors. White couches glow in their minimalist surroundings like the ones at an Ian Schrager hotel. After lunch Vittorio sat me in a room with French doors opening up on the Milanello campus. "Wait here," he told me. Two days earlier, in Manchester, Milan had won their sixth European Champions League title, sealed in penalty kicks after 120 minutes of scoreless soccer. As I waited for Vittorio, Milan's tri-umphant coach Carlo Ancelotti entered, carrying the team's massive, newly acquired trophy. He was fol-lowed by a horde of applauding maids and other Milanello employees. While he took photos with them, the team began trickling into the room. I had opened up a book and made a pretense of reading. But in truth Vittorio had stage-managed a scene that most Italian men would have killed to watch. A parade of the world's greatest players—Manuel Rui Costa, Paolo Maldini,

Alessandro Nesta—walked up to me and shook my hand. They took turns hugging Ancelotti and lifting the cup. They were in an exuberant mood, and, after my brief interactions with these gods of football, so was I.

I went to find Vittorio, who was sitting at the team's bar drinking another coffee.

"One favor. Can I go to tomorrow night's game? Can you help me get a credential or ticket?" I desperately wanted to see Milan play in their futuristic home stadium, the San Siro. And the next evening they played Roma in the finals of the Coppa Italia, a year-long tournament that yields the second most important title in the country.

"Come on!" he told me, shrugging his shoulders. "The AC Milan press office can get you whatever you want."

While nobody can be sure how Juventus gets such nice treatment from referees, soccer pundits have a good sense of how Milan does it: It manipulates the press. The club is famous for the sort of openness that they gave me. Where Juventus only reluctantly lets its players speak to reporters, and sometimes not even that, Milan releases its team to schmooze for hours. Even Berlusconi, famously distant from political reporters, will always field questions about his beloved Milan. Standing with Israeli president Ariel Sharon, fresh from a discussion about Mid-East peace, Berlusconi once began talking about his lack of interest in buying David Beckham from Manchester United.

I've traveled with the White House and American presidential campaigns, but not even Karl Rove and Karen Hughes play the media with the skill of Milan.

When I went to the Coppa Italia finals, a press officer greeted me at a gate with a ticket. She kissed me on both cheeks and promised to keep tabs on me. The Milan press box, midfield in open air, truly gives the scribblers the best seats in the house. Pretty women in blazers with the Milan insignia—there were about as many of them as reporters—continually pass through the box, like stewardesses on an airliner, asking after your comfort.

As a television man, Berlusconi has always been obsessed with surface appearance and seduction of the audience. This is why he labors so assiduously to maintain a year-round suntan, and why he wears double-breasted suits perfectly tailored to obscure his Napoleonic stature. At the Milanello training ground, the head of the facility spoke to me at great length about Berlusconi's interest in the minute details of landscaping. He had insisted on the rose garden and ordered the terraces. When he comes to visit, the landscaping crew removes the cars from the front lot so that Berlusconi can more fully enjoy the beauty of the grounds.

But this aestheticism is merely one feature of Berlusconi's knack for producing great spectacle—a hallmark of the new oligarchs. This talent can be witnessed in AC Milan, his greatest spectacle of all. Although the team still isn't as offensive-minded as the specimens that can be found in Latin America or Spain, Milan represents a major break with the long Italian history of defensive-minded *catenaccio*. When Berlusconi bought the club in the mid-eighties, he imported Dutchmen like Marco Van Basten and the dreadlocked Ruud Gullit and Frank Rijkaard, players with an irrepressible instinct to move forward in attack. The whole team was built to entertain and play a brand of soccer more beautiful than anything Juventus could deliver. And in the end, it delivered Champions League titles and Scudettos, the Italian championship trophy.

Sitting in the San Siro, watching the finals of the Coppa Italia, I had a glimpse of how powerful and touching this spectacle can be. After the match, when the team had already racked up its second major trophy of the week, the lights in the stadium went dim. The darkness highlighted the flares that *ultras*—the highly organized, highly enthusiastic members of fan clubs—lofted above their heads, spewing red smoke. Lasers focused a twirling image of the team's cursive name and the European Cup hardware on the field. As classic rock anthems blared, with fans singing along, each player trotted onto the field through an inflatable tunnel. The crowd would break from their singing to shout their names as they emerged. All around me, grown men grew teary. I'm told that this moment, as moving as I found it, couldn't touch the truly epic spectacles that Berlusconi has produced over the years. Most famously, there was the episode dubbed "Apocalypse Now." After Berlusconi bought the club, he introduced it by flying his players into the stadium on helicopters, with Wagner's "Ride of the Valkyries" blaring in the background.

At nearly every juncture in my dealings with Milan, I felt the organization's manipulative touch. But why spend so much time trying to shape the opinions of the press? In Rome, I met a man called Mario Sconcerti who explained the importance of winning over the media. Sconcerti has come at the issue from both sides. He had edited the *Corriere dello Sport,* one of two daily national papers devoted largely to the coverage of soccer. In 2001, he went on to run the day-to-day operations of the club Fiorentina, one of the more storied outfits in Italy. In his elegant, airy Roman apartment, interspersed among his floor-to-ceiling collection of modern art, he has a framed photo of angry Fiorentina fans holding up a banner filled with expletives directed at him.

Sconcerti has a reputation as a rebel in the chummy world of Italian soccer, a man who has just enough ego to speak truthfully about the power of the Agnellis and Berlusconi. Besides, he's from Florence, and Florentines are famously skeptical about the fact that AC Milan and Juventus have won so many championships, while their home team always seemed to be falling just short. If Sconcerti weren't so respected, I would have found his view of the Italian game highly conspiratorial and too intricate to be plausible, the expression of his ticks and biases.

By Sconcerti's estimate, the press can be manipulated to increase a team's total by as much as six points, the difference between a championship and second place. Once again, the manipulation hinges on pressure exerted on referees. He argues that the media can either turn away from or expose the preferential treatment that referees give to Juventus and Milan. If the press launches a crusade against a referee, it makes the referee extremely self-conscious. He will bend over backwards to avoid appearing biased, and may unconsciously bend even further than that.

Watching Italian television, and shows like *Il Processo,* it is possible to see precisely how the media brings itself to bear on the refs. Sconcerti has done some of this manipulation himself. During the 2000 season, Sconcerti's paper launched a campaign on behalf of Roma and Lazio. Every day, the *Corriere dello Sport* would rail against the favoritism shown to Berlusconi's and Agnelli's clubs. And at a certain point, Sconcerti and many others believe, they could see that the referees become more generous to Lazio and Roma. In 2000 and 2001 seasons, he humbly points out, the Roman teams won national championships. This is the rare opportunity when somebody has dared quantify the value of press manipulation. With Milan, it's nearly impossible to pick out the areas where Berlusconi's spin machine has produced favorable treatment. Sconcerti, however, is convinced that it exists. As we sat in his apartment and drank sparkling water, he listed the referees who have been hired by Berlusconi's television networks as commentators, and the referees criticized on them.

It is easy to believe the worst about Berlusconi, in both soccer and life. But in part, Berlusconi raises suspicions because he doesn't fit the classic archetype of the Italian elite. This can be seen from the start of his biography. In Italy nobody works summer jobs between school semesters, especially if they don't need a salary to stave off starvation. Even though Berlusconi hailed from a middle-class family, he paid his way through college and law school by toiling on his vacations, running a business that booked bands for cruise ships. When he couldn't find other acts, he crooned himself, cultivating a Frank Sinatra persona. As an entrepreneur, he always had a penchant for following an American model. He made his first major fortune building a suburb for yuppies outside Milan. His television empire owed its vast reach to the steady diet of *Dallas* and *Falcon Crest* that Berlusconi fed his audience.

While Berlusconi had been a major media mogul before becoming a sports mogul, it was the purchase of the soccer club in 1986 that launched him to national prominence. When he entered politics in 1994, running for prime minister, the game undergirded his electoral strategy. In a matter of months, Berlusconi's advertising firm Publitalia (one of his breathtaking array of holdings) went about the business of building him a political party. For the party's base, it started with the several million fans of AC Milan. It converted supporters' clubs into local headquarters for his party. Publitalia filched the party's name from a soccer chant, "Forza Italia"—"Go Italy!" In party literature, Publitalia dubbed the Forza Italia rank and file the "Azuri," the same nickname given to the players on the national team for their blue uniforms.

Berlusconi invoked soccer so relentlessly because his club was in the middle of a spectacular run that included consecutive Champions League titles. He wanted to plant the idea in voters' minds that he was a winner, at a time when the economy sputtered and all politicians in Italy seemed like corrupt losers. "We will make Italy like Milan," he tirelessly repeated. There was also a populist brilliance to his use of soccer as a metaphor for society. It gave him a vocabulary that resonated with the lower middle class, the group that he wanted to cultivate as a political base. Explaining the rationale for his candidacy, he told voters, "I heard that the game was getting dangerous and it was being played in the two penalty areas, with the midfield being left desolately empty."

Franco, Mussolini, and a high percentage of all modern dictators have made the link between sport and populist politics countless times. To Berlusconi's left-wing critics, the resemblance to these tyrants is not coincidental. He is their scion. Like the Latin American caudillos, they say, he is thoroughly corrupted. At the same time he has assumed responsibility for governing Italy, he has maintained a vast business empire that profits from the state's largess and reluctance to regulate. Predictably, when his personal interests conflict with the commonweal, he backs himself. Despite serious allegations about his own corruption, in 2003 he orchestrated the passage of legislation granting himself blanket immunity from prosecution. He has decriminalized the offense of false accounting, which his company is accused of committing.

His soccer dealings have the same taint. He may not be making Agnelli-like behind-the-scenes overtures to referees and politicians, but the system always looks stacked to promote his interests. In soccer, Berlusconi's deputy at AC Milan, Adriano Galliani, has become the chairman of the Italian league—with a portfolio that includes the meting of discipline and the negotiation of television rights.

In the United States, the case against Berlusconi might be too much for the polity to tolerate. But in Italy, the electorate doesn't penalize Berlusconi for his conflicts of interest. This brand of corruption is too widespread to be pinned on a single man. The critics who point out his conflicts sound like hypocrites. They don't want a world with media beholden only to journalistic truth and objectivity. They idealize the days when the Socialists and Christian Democrats each controlled one of the state-run television networks. Nobody, on either side of the spectrum, has any real interest in rationalizing government contracts, the prime vehicle for corruption.

Taking into account this consensus against reform, it's hard to single out Berlusconi for rage. Compared to the old oligarchy's back channels, Berlusconi manipulates in the wide-open, as he does with AC Milan's press operation. In 2003, when he pushed the legislature to pass a law granting him blanket immunity from prosecution, Italians could follow the proceedings in their newspapers and on television. A few activists took to the streets, but only a small sliver of Italy cared.

IV.

One rainy night I met up with Tommaso Pellizzari, a young reporter with the newspaper *Corriere della Sera* and rabid fan of AC Milan's fierce cross-town rival, Inter. I searched out Tommaso because he is one of the most vociferous critics of Berlusconi's club. In 2001, he published a polemic called *No Milan,* modeled after Naomi Klein's anti-globalization tract *No Logo.* The book is a clever, somewhat jokey, mostly rageful attack on all things Milan. It lists the ten all-time Milan players he hates most—and the ten he likes most, because they affirm the inferiority of their club.

His charming argument finishes with a counter-intuitive flourish. In the last chapter, Pellizzari admits gratitude for Berlusconi's ownership of his enemy. To most Inter fans, this confession would be anathema. Berlusconi's essentially bottomless bank accounts have financed an implacable foe. But Pellizzari cares as much about the soul and moral health of his club as he does championships. And thanks to Berlusconi's association with AC Milan, he argues, Italians can no longer turn a blind eye to the wickedness of Milan. It has become objectively odious. Indeed, Pellizzari sees a "boomerang effect." Italians have rallied against AC Milan, because they see the club as a symbol of the corrupt, conservative regime.

Broadly speaking, there's not much evidence of the boomerang arcing back toward Milan. In fact, the opposite has happened. Because of Berlusconi's glamour players and championship trophies, Milan has developed a national following that may soon eclipse Juventus's broad base. In certain intellectual circles, however, Milan has become just as despised as Tommaso hoped. To illustrate this point, he took me to a bohemian theater and cultural club called Comuna Baires. Ever since Berlusconi returned to power in 2001, the Comuna Baires has formed an alliance with Inter Milan. It hosts literary evenings with the team. At its readings, foreign Inter players (from Colombia, Turkey, and so on) share the stage with writers from their home countries. After the events, Inter players, coaches, and team officials join pro-Inter intellectuals for dinner around a long table in the theater's basement. It's the type of evening that could only happen with Italian leftists, who have been nursed on Antonio Gramsci and his theories of counter-hegemony.

The evening Tommaso and I attended Comuna Baires, the club held a reading to honor Javier Zanetti, Inter's Argentine captain. Everyone in the club seemed to know Tommaso. A camera crew from Inter's cable television network stopped him for a quick interview. Beautiful women in black stopped to kiss him on both cheeks. We dropped our coats in a cloakroom, away from the crowd. Tommaso whispered to me, "I have to warn you. These people really are communists. I don't mean that as an exaggeration. They really are communists." We walked out from the room and he nudged me, nodding toward a framed picture of Che Guevara that stared at us from a wooden beam.

Like any boho theater, the Baires has a ramshackle feel. The main stage is in a stark black room with risers and rickety wooden benches. The reading had been organized in the round and a row of men and women in tiny spectacles surrounded Zanetti. He sat in front of a microphone at a table, draped with cloth the colors of Inter's jersey. Waiting for the program to begin, he shifted in his seat.

The theater's director emceed the evening. A middle-aged man in an untucked linen shirt, he warmed up the audience with an impassioned stem-winder about Inter. He praised the club for its "anti-Bush, anti-Berlusconi, anti-American" worldview. To justify this claim, he cited the club's long record of falling just short of winning championships. In contrast to the ethic of American capitalism, Inter fans know that there are "things more important in life than winning."

A parade of journalists and novelists and poets followed him to the microphone, each paying tribute to Inter and Zanetti, many taking the same anti-capitalist line as the emcee. Between speakers, the director handed Zanetti oil paintings that had been created in his honor.

There were certain contradictions in this effort to superimpose a left-wing identity on Inter. First of all, it doesn't make any sense to link the club to the anti-globalization movement. An oil magnate owns Inter. Although he has center-left sympathies, and has even flirted with a political career, he runs Inter in the unabashed spirit of capitalism. Then, when they try to graft cosmopolitanism onto this club, they fail miserably. They can never get past the fact that Inter represents the petite bourgeoisie of northern Italy, a group that resents immigration more than any in the country. The stands of Inter games contain far more racist chants and banners than they do for Berlusconi's club.

This is certainly not the first instance of irrationalism and inconsistency on the Italian left. More than any country in Western Europe, Italians have indulged a romantic politics. Where the show trials of the '30s, the Hitler-Stalin non-aggression pact, the crushing of the Hungarian uprising, and the fall of the Berlin Wall turned off most of humanity to communism, the Italian enthusiasm for Karl Marx's doctrine never really abated. They kept faith with the Communist Party into the 1990s, even though the party kept mouthing crusty words about revolution and the dictatorship of the

proletariat. This wasn't a small segment of the electorate. Communists routinely received close to a third
of the vote.

And there's another plague that curses the Italian
left, a tendency toward snobbery. They've turned
Berlusconi and Milan into a bigger villain than Agnelli
and Juventus, because Berlusconi couldn't be more
déclassé. As one newspaper columnist told me, "He
imports low-brow American TV shows and movies; he
tells dirty jokes and commits ridiculous gaffes." An
important investigation into the genesis of his empire
was called *The Odor of Money*. But his real curse, it
sometime seems, is to have the odor of new money.

The left's apoplectic reaction to Berlusconi undermines its ability to combat him. Instead of satisfying
the Italian craving for spectacle, his opponents are gray
politicians, usually with academic pedigrees and mild-
mannered demeanors. (Berlusconi's archenemy,
Romano Prodi, for instance, makes a point of touting
his own devotion to cycling, a sport that doesn't have
near the mass following of football.) They keep hitting
Berlusconi for crimes that have already been exposed
and, for better or worse, excused by the electorate. Like
the Inter intellectuals, they seem ludicrously discon-
nected from the reality of their potential supporters.

At dinner, Tommaso and I sat across the table from
Zanetti. He couldn't have been more appreciative or
happier to be at the table. "Where are you from?" he
asked me in Spanish. As we made pleasant, perfunc-
tory chitchat, the table erupted into a voluble debate on
the merits of past Inter squads. The intellectuals were
especially prone to celebrating the mystical qualities

and aesthetic sensibilities of players, in the same manner they had championed Zanetti earlier in the
evening. Sitting on the fringe of this conversation,
Zanetti listened intently, looking over the shoulder of
other participants. At first, he tentatively tried to inter-
ject himself into the conversation, providing illustrative
first-hand observations about playing for Inter. But
these interventions weren't heard, as far as I could tell,
over the din. Debating Inter's heroes of the past, the
table ignored the Inter hero of the present they had just
celebrated in such glowing terms. After a few minutes,
Zanetti gave up on the conversation and focused on
quickly finishing the pizza on his plate. The hero politely
excused himself, gathered his paintings, and fled.

8

How Soccer Explains the Discreet Charm of Bourgeois Nationalism

I.

The motto of FC Barcelona is *"mas que un club,"* more than a club. For the purposes of full disclosure, I agree. It's more than a club; it's one of God's greatest gifts to leisure time. I wrote that last sentence while wearing a Barca cap and a frayed replica jersey that I bought ten years ago. Later today, I'll pretend to write this chapter while constantly refreshing my browser for updates of Barca's game against Newcastle United in the Champions League. And tonight, I'll have a dream about a long curving pass from Xavi that will be met by Javier Saviola after the little man unbelievably crosses a large swath of grass. Even if the rules of reality have been suspended, it's too much of a stretch to imagine myself on the field with Saviola. But I will still picture myself in the scene, in the lower tier of the Camp Nou, Barca's stadium.

With the rest of the stadium, I will be singing Saviola's name like a Gregorian chant, exaggerating each syllable for maximum haunting effect. The person sitting next to me will be flying a ten-foot Catalan flag above my head.

Barca became my team in 1994 on a winter trip through the city. My visit coincided with the annual gratis opening of Barca's museum. It is the most visited museum in the city, even ahead of a massive collection of Picasso canvases. With no admission fee, lines crawled across the stadium parking lot, filled with eight-year-old boys and their mothers, silver-haired men paying a visit to old friends in the trophy case, and teenage girls apparently brushing up on team history. The transcendent enthusiasm for a bunch of artifacts and sepia photos moved me. I felt like a nonbeliever watching a religious pilgrimage. And the sheer depth of their faith made me a believer, too.

If you have liberal politics and yuppie tastes, it isn't easy to find a corner of the soccer firmament that feels like home. The continent has too many clubs that have freaky fascist pasts bleeding into a xenophobic present. And this is only the first obstacle to finding a team. You could never accept clubs with a cloud of virulent racism trailing after them. (Remove from the list of potential favorites, then, Paris Saint-Germain, Chelsea, Glasgow Rangers, Red Star Belgrade, and almost half the teams in Italy.) And for the sake of the underdog, you couldn't possibly abide the multinational conglomerates, like Manchester United and Juventus, which buy championships every year.

Barca elegantly fills this vacuum. Over the course of its history, it has self-consciously announced its sophistication. The Barca museum houses paintings by Dali and Miro. Outside its front gate, it displays modern sculpture, ranging from Donald Judd–like minimalism to neo-futurism. A disciple of Le Corbusier designed the roof of its old grounds.

I've heard, but never confirmed, a theory that the club explicitly plucked its colors—red and blue—from the tricolor of the French revolution. If not true in fact, the story has a spiritual truth. Indeed, the team's modernist aesthetic flows from its leftist politics. At the height of the 1930s anarchism fad, Barca became a worker's collective, a legacy that continues. Its season ticket holders still vote for the club's administration, with presidential debates broadcast live on television and candidates making impossibly grand campaign promises to purchase a team of superstar players. More important, according to the lore of the institution, the club was the heroic center of the resistance to Franco's military dictatorship. Only the Camp Nou provided Catalans a place to yell and scream against the regime in their own, banned vernacular. Manuel Vazquez Montalban, one of Spain's great contemporary writers, published a novel about Barca called *Offside*. He described the club as "the epic weapon of a country without a state.... El Barca's victories were like those of Athens over Sparta."

Even now in more placid times, a charming fervor surrounds the club's politics. Government officials expound on affairs of club as if they were affairs of state. At various moments, the longtime president of Catalonia, Jordi Pujol, recommended changes of lineup, strategic formation, and recruiting tactics. The major

Catalan political parties form stealth alliances with the candidates for the Barca presidency, in hopes that the Barca president will invite party leaders to sit in the Camp Nou's tribune of honor in the center of the stadium.

Because of this sense of mission, the club makes fantastic gestures to prove its purity, to show that it resides on a higher plane than the base world of commerce. Of all the clubs in the world, only Barcelona has no advertisements covering the front of its jersey. Until 2003, the club refused even to entertain offers to buy this sacred space. When the highest paid players in the world—Maradona, Ronaldo, Rivaldo—demonstrate insufficient enthusiasm for the cause, Barca and its fans turn on them. They send them to another city, despite the many goals they have scored for the team. If a coach adopts utilitarian tactics that skimp on artistry, he gets sacked, no matter the trophies he has accumulated. Supporters of Barca want nothing more badly than victory, except for romance. And as the club's long history of underachieving shows, they get far more of the latter.

Unfortunately, large swaths of the world don't fully appreciate these many splendors of Barca. More than Real Madrid and Manchester United, richer teams that win far more championships, Barca provokes irk and ire. I've had Serb translators and Croatian friends bridge the deepest divides and shout their mutual hatred of Barca. I've witnessed Israeli academics and Muslim taxi drivers unknowingly form a union of schadenfreude when Barca self-destructs. I guess I can understand the sentiment. *"Mas que un club"* implies superiority. The pious refusal to turn its jersey into a billboard damns the business decisions made by every other club to stay afloat. The modern art and the novels may seem too precious by half. Soccer should be watched with beer and burgers, perhaps, not cappuccino and cigarettes.

But if Barca's enemies objectively considered the club they despise, they would find an important reason to stand up and bathe it in applause. Critics of soccer contend that the game inherently culminates in death and destruction. They argue that the game gives life to tribal identities which should be disappearing in a world where a European Union and globalization are happily shredding such ancient sentiments. Another similar widely spread thesis holds that the root cause of violence can be found in the pace of the game itself. Because goals come so irregularly, fans spend far too much time sublimating their emotions, anticipating but not ever releasing. When those emotions swell and become uncontainable, the fans erupt into dark, Dionysian fits of ecstatic violence.

Barca redeems the game from these criticisms, by showing that fans can love a club and a country with passion and without turning into a thug or terrorist. Sure, its fans can ascend to the highest levels of irrationality—positing wild conspiracies, imagining their own victimhood, and pitting themselves against supposedly existential enemies. Yet they almost never cross into the darker realms of human behavior. There are no opposing fans that Barca considers subhuman and hardly any violence associated with the club. Its stadium is filled with more women and children than any in Europe. It is also filled with immigrants from the south of Spain, who affiliate with the club to ease their assimilation into Catalan life.

Put more strongly, Barca doesn't just redeem the game from its critics; it redeems the concept of nationalism. Through the late twentieth century, liberal political thinkers, from the philosopher Martha Nussbaum to the architects of the European Union, have blamed nationalism for most of modernity's evils. Tribalism in a more modern guise, they denounce it. If only we abandoned this old fixation with national identities, then we could finally get past nasty ethnocentrism, vulgar chauvinism, and blood feuding. In place of nationalism, they propose that we become cosmopolitans—shelving patriotism and submitting to government by international institutions and laws.

It's a beautiful picture, but not at all realistic. And it turns its back on a strain of liberalism that begins with John Stuart Mill and Alexis de Tocqueville and continues through Isaiah Berlin. This tradition understands that humans crave identifying with a group. It is an unavoidable, immemorial, hardwired instinct. Since modern life has knocked the family and tribe from their central positions, the nation has become the only viable vessel for this impulse. To deny this craving is to deny human nature and human dignity.

What's more, this strain of political theory makes a distinction between liberal nationalism and illiberal nationalism. The Serbs at Red Star, to take the most obvious example, practice the illiberal variety, with no respect for the determination of other nationalities. But there's no reason that nationalism should inherently culminate in these ugly feelings. To blame the Croatian and Bosnian wars on excessive love of country drastically underestimates the pathologies in Serb culture. Besides, in theory, patriotism and cosmopolitanism should be perfectly compatible. You could love your country—even consider it a superior group—without desiring to dominate other groups or closing yourself off to foreign impulses. And it's not just theory. This is the spirit of Barca. I love it.

II.

FC Barcelona could have easily gone the other direction. It could have become a caldron of radicalism, violence, and grievances. But the roots of Barca's cosmopolitan nationalism run too deep. They are part of the national culture and part of the club's founding spirit. In 1899, a Swiss Protestant businessman called Joan Gamper joined with English expats to launch FC Barcelona. It is stunning that a foreigner created what would become a defining institution of Catalan nationalism.

There's a simple explanation for Catalonia's openness to foreign influences: Catalonia sits in the middle of the Mediterranean world. Before the fifteenth century, as part of the kingdom of Aragon, the Catalan conquered their way as far east as Athens, Sicily, and Sardinia. Even then, at the height of its greatness, the nation's most powerful men were traders and capitalists. Barcelona became a great trading city deeply entangled in the global economy, growing into an industrial giant. By the late nineteenth century, only the United States,

England, and France outpaced the production of Catalonia's textile mills.

But as it advanced economically, Catalonia sustained political subjugation. Spain's political power, concentrated in Madrid, consisted largely of Castilian landowners. The interests of the central government and Barcelona's capitalists clashed. Barcelona's growing cadre of bourgeois nationalists resented that the Castilians used the government to impose "Spanish" culture and language upon them. Nor did it help that Madrid tilted government policy so strongly away from industry and toward the protection of agriculture. The Catalans took out their anger at this unjust arrangement by crudely stereotyping the Castilians and their capital. Where Catalonia represented modernity and progress, Madrid consisted of cultureless yokels. It wasn't entirely a self-serving image. Barcelona's bourgeoisie proved its greatness to the world, by patronizing monumental works of art and architecture—Gaudí, Doménech i Muntaner, Miró. And because of its immersion in the world of global commerce, it happily opened the doors to foreign influences.

Joan Gamper and soccer were just another of the imports to become part of the Catalan fabric. It didn't hurt Gamper's local image that he fervently admired the Catalan cause and had translated his own name, Hans Kamper, into the local language. By some accounts, Gamper wanted the club to celebrate the Catalans and their dreams of autonomy. Under his stewardship, Barca adopted a crest containing the colors of the nation and the cross of St. Jordi, Catalonia's patron.

Catalonia's proclamations of national superiority didn't go down well in Madrid. The ancient Castilian regime tried to put the upstarts in their place. With the support of the king, in 1923, general Miguel Primo de Rivera seized power and ran a dictatorship that prefigured the Francoism to come. Primo de Rivera banned the Catalan flag and purged the Catalan language from the public sphere. Because of its symbolic role, Barca inevitably faced the same repression. After its fans booed the national anthem before a 1925 exhibition game, the dictator shuttered Barca's stadium for six months and fined its directors. The government made it clear to Gamper that he should leave Spain or his family might suffer some unfortunate consequences. Gamper fled. A few years later, in a fit of depression, compounded by his losses in the 1929 stock market crash, he took his own life.

Primo de Rivera had Franco's agenda without Franco's totalitarian state apparatus to back him up. Rather predictably his repression backfired. He resigned in 1930, replaced by a democratic republic imbued with the utopian fervor of the interwar era. There was, however, an important difference between Franco's attitude and his forerunner. Primo de Rivera had reacted to Barca with fury because he was a classic caudillo, your run-of-the-mill dictator who squashed any dissent that threatened his fragile grip. For Franco, the battle against Barca took on the form of epic personal struggle. On the most obvious political level, he had good reason for punishing the club's devoted supporters. Catalonia had held out the longest against his coup. Barcelonans, after years of pre–civil war industrial strife, had become Henry Fords of barricade construction. Although parts of the city welcomed Franco with open arms, many of its residents fought urban warfare with a savvy that Che Guevara could never equal. Franco extracted a price for this resistance. When the city fell, Franco killed unknown numbers of them and buried them in a mass grave on Montjuic hill, the future home of the Olympic stadium.

But there was another, equally important reason for Franco's hatred for Barca. The Generalissimo followed the game obsessively, and, more specifically, he followed Barca's rival, Real Madrid obsessively. He could recite Real lineups going back decades and let it be known that he relaxed in his palace by watching the game of the week on television. (Not coincidentally state TV featured Real Madrid in its weekly broadcast far more than any other team.) When he watched, he even had a stake in the outcome. Franco liked to play a state-sponsored pool that allowed him to place bets on soccer.

Franco prosecuted his personal vendetta against Barca to the fullest. Manuel Vazquez Montalban has written, "Franco's occupying troops entered the city, fourth on the list of organizations to be purged, after the Communists, the Anarchists and the Separatists, was Barcelona Football Club." At the start of Franco's three-year revolt, fascist gendarmes arrested and then executed Barca's left-leaning president Josep Sunyol as he drove across the Guadarrama hills to visit Catalan troops guarding Madrid against a right-wing siege. When Franco's troops made a final push to conquer obstreperous Catalonia, they bombed the building that held the club's trophies. After demolishing the club's hardware, the Francoists set out to strip it of its identity. The regime insisted on changing "Football Club Barcelona" to "Club de Football Barcelona"—not a tiny aesthetic point, but the translation of the team's name into Castilian Spanish. It also insisted on purging the Catalan flag from the team crest. And these were only Franco's opening salvos. To oversee the ideological transformation of the club, the regime installed a new president. He should have been well suited to the task. During the war, he had been captain of the civil guard's "Anti-Marxist Division." At Barca, he carefully kept thick police files on everyone involved with the club, so that he could impede and undermine any officials with latent nationalist sympathies.

During these early years of the Franco era, one event jumps from the history books. In 1943, Barca played Real in the semifinals of the Generalissimo's Cup. Moments before game time, the director of state security entered Barca's locker room—a scene enshrined in the journalist Jimmy Burns's magisterial history of the club, *Barca*. He reminded the players that many of them had only just returned to Spain from wartime exile thanks to an amnesty excusing their flight. "Do not forget that some of you are only playing because of the generosity of the regime that has forgiven your lack of patriotism." In those recrimination-filled years, the hint wasn't hard to take. Barca lost the match 11–1, one of the most lopsided defeats in team history.

This was the first of many favors the regime granted to Real Madrid, which seemed to return the affection by placing its new stadium on the Avenida de

Generalissimo Franco. According to some, the regime
gave decisive aid to Real Madrid in its signing of the
best player of the fifties, the Argentine Alfredo Di Ste-
fano, even though Barca had already agreed to terms
with him. When Real Madrid won championships,
Franco bestowed medals on the club and honorifics not
granted other winners. Paul Preston, the caudillo's
biographer, wrote, "Franco saw the triumphs of Real
Madrid and of the Spanish national team as somehow
his own." All this is fact. But there's a way in which
these facts don't add up to quite the anti-Barca conspir-
acy that Catalans present. One significant detail gets in
the way. In the early years of the Franco era, Barca experienced one of the better runs in its history.

It's a paradox—repression and triumph—and
leads to one of the thorniest questions in the political
history of the game. Umberto Eco has phrased it this
way: "Is it possible to have a revolution on football Sunday?" For Barca this subject sits especially uncomfort-
ably. Its fans like to brag that their stadium gave them a
space to vent their outrage against the regime. Embold-
ened by 100,000 people chanting in unison, safety in
numbers, fans seized the opportunity to scream things
that could never be said, even furtively, on the street or
in the café. This is a common enough phenomenon.
There's a long history of resistance movements igniting
in the soccer stadium. In the Red Star Revolution,
Draza, Krle, and the other Belgrade soccer hooligans
helped topple Slobodan Milosevic. Celebrations for
Romania's 1990 World Cup qualification carried over
into the Bucharest squares, culminating in a firing
squad that trained its rifles on the dictator Nicolae

Ceausescu and his wife. The movement that toppled the Paraguayan dictator Alfredo Stroessner had the same sportive ground zero.

But when Barca fans proudly point to Camp Nou's subversive spirit, they can't satisfactorily explain why Franco didn't just squash it. Of course, he could have easily. He ran an efficient police state, where both the trains and the grand inquisitors ran on time. To crack down on Barca, as Primo de Rivera had done in the 1920s, would have required few troops. But he set this option to the side and he chose to let the partisans scream their obscenities against him. Franco never explicitly justified this policy of tolerance. But its purpose was clear enough: to let the Catalan people channel their political energies into a harmless pastime.

If Barca let Catalonia blow off steam, it turned out to be a tidy arrangement for all involved. Franco never faced any serious opposition from the Catalans. Unlike the Basques, the other linguistic minority suffering under Franco, the Catalans never joined liberation fronts or kidnapped Madrid bank presidents or exploded bombs at bus stations. And Barca supporters, for all their noise in the Camp Nou, never seriously objected to the Franco apologists who ruled the club's boardroom. While Catalonia kept its head down, it got on with business. Franco's nationalist economics, which included subsidies and tariffs, abetted a massive industrial boom in metropolitan Barcelona. Immigrants from the south of Spain, many thousands in the fifties and sixties, came to work the region's factories. The new industrial strength and concomitant wealth helped take the mind off oppression and memories of slaughter.

Catalans have a self-description that explains this temperamental instinct toward going along. They like to say that they possess a national quality called *seny,* a word that translates into something in between pragmatism and canniness. It's the legacy from their centuries as Mediterranean traders, a businessman's aversion to trouble. (A classic example of *seny:* Catalans insist that their language be taught in universities and deployed on street signs. It can be found everywhere, except the real estate sections of many Catalan-language newspapers. Nationalism shouldn't ever obstruct a deal.) In this self-description, the Catalans also admit that they possess a yin to the *seny* yang. They have another national characteristic called *rauxa,* a tendency toward violent outbursts. This characteristic propelled Catalonia to fight so determinedly during the Spanish Civil War and made it so pugilistic in the years before.

Whether by Franco's design or not, Barca helped to preserve Catalonia's *seny* and *rauxa* in a state of comfortable equilibrium. A sportswriter told me a parable that illustrates this point. Two criminals, locked away in one of Franco's prisons, execute a perfectly planned break. They time their escape so that they can watch Barca play Real Madrid in the Camp Nou. As good fortune would have it, the liberated watch their beloved Barca triumph. They have both freedom and victory. From here, they had simply to follow the script provided by dozens of buddy movies and hit the road. But they performed their roles as Catalan men, not Hollywood actors. Cured of their *rauxa* by Barca, they retrace their steps to the building where they had suffered for so long. They seek out a warden and turn themselves in.

III.

There's a thin line between passion and madness. The former Barcelona striker Hristo Stoichkov constantly crosses it. As a teenager in Bulgaria, he once instigated a massive mid-game brawl. His performance that day was so violent, so feral and uncontrolled, that the Bulgarian soccer federation banned him from the game for life. But he was too good and too adored to suffer this fate. When the Bulgarian public complained that it had been deprived of a great hero, the federation downgraded the punishment to a year's suspension. With maturity, his violent outbursts never really abated. In four years at Barca, referees tossed him from 11 games. He would not only put himself in the faces of referees, he would stomp on their toes. A few months before I went to visit him in Washington, D.C., where he played last season, he had just scrimmaged against college kids, a meaningless "friendly" match. But Stoichkov has only a limited ability to modulate his style, and the notion of friendly has no cognitive resonance with him. In the game, he slid into a freshman from behind with both his legs turned up, so hard that he snapped the player's bones. The sound of cracking traveled across the field. On the sideline, spectators and players retched.

Reducing Stoichkov to his temper, however, sells him short. He isn't without incredible appeal. A poll once found him the most popular Barca player of all time. In part, his popularity was a just reward for performance. Between 1990 and 1994, he scored 104 goals for the club. His eccentric playing persona, in turns delicate and brutal, contributed massively to Barca's *annus mirablis,* including its lone Champions League title. In 1994, he won European Player of the Year. Catalans also worshipped Stoichkov, because he replicated their passion—and the unreasonable expectations, unfair demands, and hypercriticism that come with such passion. "My colleagues are lazy, dumb and money hungry," he once complained. Like the Catalans, Stoichkov believed that Barca should be playing for the cause and not a paycheck.

Only a few native Catalan players have more enthusiastically championed the political ideology of the club or the country. It goes beyond the requisite hatred for Real Madrid, although Stoichkov has expressed his disdain with singular intensity. ("I will always hate Real Madrid," he once said. "I would rather the ground opened up and took me under than accept a job with them. In fact, I really do not like speaking about them because when I do it makes me want to vomit.") He has a fanatical devotion to Catalonian nationalism. When Bulgaria played Spain in the 1998 World Cup, he hung a Catalan flag from the balcony of his hotel. He promised that he would wear a T-shirt beneath his jersey agitating for secession from Spain. These gestures, much hyped and appreciated in Barcelona, only culminated a personal history of rabid Catalanism. He has been a leader in a campaign for Catalonia to withdraw its support for the Spanish national squad and to field its own separate team at the

World Cup. Barcelona papers have reported that he has endorsed the Party for Catalonian Independence—strangely placing himself left of the mainstream of Catalan nationalism.

Stoichkov proves the inclusiveness of Catalan nationalism, its greatest virtue. It welcomes, even worships, foreigners. Barca's history is full of foreign players—Scotsmen, Hungarians, Dutchmen—who have taken up residence in the city and become proponents of the club's politics. (Dutch great Johan Cruyff named his Barcelona-born son Jordi, possibly the first Franco-era baby with this Catalan first name.) The foreigners can become Catalan, because the ideology of Catalanism holds that citizenship is acquired, not inherited. To become Catalan, one must simply learn the Catalan language, disparage Castilian Spain, and love Barca. Catalan nationalism is not a racial doctrine or theocratic one, but a thoroughly civic religion. Catalan nationalism is so blind that it will accept you even if you have an impossible personality.

Getting an interview with Stoichkov is not easy. After weeks of putting me off, he agreed to meet after practice in the locker room of his club, D.C. United. Stoichkov sat on a chair fresh from a shower, wearing a terry cloth robe with a hood. To amuse his teammates, he pulled the hood over his head, jumped out of his chair, and mimed the motions of a boxer preparing to fight. There was a wild quality to his drama. He threw hard punches in the air and bounced into naked guys as if he were going to pound them. When he returned to his chair, I sat down beside him and began to introduce myself.

"In Spanish," he said. "Much better in Spanish."

"Bueno. Yo soy . . ."

I realized that Stoichkov made me too nervous to ask questions in Spanish. He blurts out his phrases and has perfected the tough man's look that seems menacing even in the nude. He wears a permanent coat of stubble over gaunt cheeks. His most innocuous movements look like wind-ups to a punch.

I asked the team's press handler for some help. He recruited the team's equipment manager to translate. Clearly, our interview would be a disaster. But I had spent too much time negotiating logistics to waste the opportunity. As I began to explain my project, Stoichkov cut me off.

"How many copies will you sell? Sharing my thoughts, will that entitle me to earn some money out of this?"

There was a long pause, during which he stared at me intently. I had no idea how to measure the seriousness of his question.

"No," I replied.

"Why not?"

"I'm a poor journalist."

He seemed very self-satisfied with his line of questioning. His responses preempted the translations. "Will you earn money?"

"Sure, maybe a little bit."

"But there are poor children in this world."

"Are you one of the poor children?" I asked.

"I'm giving you an opportunity to earn some money and we won't receive anything? I don't want the money, I won't keep the money. I'll give it to poor children. I wrote a book in Spanish and it sold 600,000 copies. Am I going to receive something or not?" I was now in the embarrassing position of having most of the team eavesdrop on our conversation.

"That's not the way that I work as a journalist," I told him.

"Would you pay Michael Jordan? Hristo Stoichkov will sell you many copies." He said that if I wrote him a check he would personally deliver the money to UNICEF. "It's not for me."

I tried to explain the practice of American journalism. "This is just not the way we do business. It's not part of our ethical system."

While I spoke, he rose and stepped into his locker. "Well, it's part of my ethical system."

"Then we can't talk?"

"No." He stripped off his robe.

We didn't shake hands. As I left the locker room, I angrily described Stoichkov's solicitation of this bribe to his press handler, who just shrugged. Because Stoichkov is a hero of Barca, I couldn't stay mad long, either. Besides, in our short exchange, he had told me nothing yet managed to encapsulate the Catalan ethos—canny about commerce alongside a streak of feistiness. And if Catalonia could find it in its heart to forgive his lunacy, so could I.

IV.

Some close followers of the game, especially in Madrid, might object to this characterization of Barcelona as a bastion of healthy, nonviolent patriotism. They will point to recent games against Real Madrid in the Camp Nou, where Barcelona fans threw projectiles on the field, including sandwiches, fruit, golf balls, mobile phones, whiskey bottles, bike chains, and a severed bloody boar's head. If there was any democratic spirit in such displays, it was the universality of this rage. Men with cigars and three-button suits, women with pearls and Escada pantsuits screamed the same obscenities, just as vulgarly and loudly as the working stiffs.

As a supporter of Barca, I can't deny these offenses. My club suffers a pathological hatred toward Real Madrid. They are the Celtic to our Rangers. But there are several key differences between this rivalry and the Scottish one. Where Celtic and Rangers cynically collude to exploit and profit from hatred, no rationality governs our ill will, no superego regulates our id. When Barcelona froths over Madrid, it moves in stupid, self-defeating directions, not financially profitable ones. Barca has a long history of underachieving, results that don't befit its all-star rosters and enormous payrolls. And this history can be attributed—at least in part—to our Real Madrid complex.

It is not easy to overestimate Real Madrid. By any measure, they are the most successful club in the sport—the New York Yankees on a continental scale. They have won more Spanish League titles than anyone. They have dominated the Champions League. Nevertheless, Barca still succeeds in giving Real Madrid far more credit than it deserves. This is their description of the politics of Spanish soccer:

A party with Francoist roots runs the Madrid city

council. To subsidize the footballers, the council bought Real Madrid's training ground from the team, paying $350 million. With one check, the city council helped finance the purchase of David Beckham, Ronaldo, and Zinedine Zedane, arguably the three best players in the world. In the Catalan view, Real's political network starts locally but extends all the way to the top. Spain's right-wing president Jose Maria Aznar has been a Real fan since his seventh birthday; he cries when the club wins championships; he dines with Real's board of directors. Because of Madrid's political connections, it gets what it wants. When Barca fans pelted Real players with the contents of their pockets, the league unjustly punished the club by making it play two home games behind closed doors, no fans allowed. "Madrid only wins championships when dictators, like Aznar and Franco, have power," the Catalan talk radio host Xavi Bosch told me.

It's a compelling portrait of power and influence, except in the details. Just as Madrid exploited a sympathetic city council, Barca has tried to do the same. But bumbling Catalan politicians have interfered with the sweetheart deal. When they describe Aznar as the new Franco, they are being highly ungrateful. For many years, Aznar included the Catalan nationalists in his governing coalition, plying them with lots of state spending and never saying a word against Catalan nationalism. Nor can they prove that Aznar has ever thrown his political weight around on behalf of his beloved club. Nevertheless, they go berserk over Aznar's sympathies. After the president dined with Real's directors, Barcelona's president demanded that he be accorded the same honor.

When Real fans hear these accusations, they say that they are symptomatic of the Catalan mau-mau. They argue that the Catalans like to cry over their "victimization" so that they can bully the central government—and the Spanish soccer federation—into giving them undeserved favors. How else can Catalonia get so much more money from the central government than any other Spanish region?

This explanation, while containing a seed of truth, lacks any empathy. Barca fans hate Madrid, because they also feel a measure of survivor's guilt. Their fathers and grandfathers suffered under the tyranny of Madrid; they died in the civil war; they couldn't speak their own language. But in the prosperity of the democratic era, Catalans have no objective basis for complaint. Their wealth and cultural renaissance should have provoked triumphalist celebrations. It hasn't, because most Catalans aren't in a mood to gloat. After witnessing their fathers' heroism, they feel as if they have lived lives devoid of struggle and without any epic dimension. They worry that their fathers would be disappointed with their staid existence.

Barca is a balm to these feelings. In its small measure, it allows Catalans to imagine they have joined the centuries-old struggle against Madrid and Castilian centralism. It lets them feel as if they, in the same way as their ancestors, have been stuck under the thumb of the arrogant imperialists. "Catalans don't want Barca to win," the journalist Joan Poqui says. "If they did, they wouldn't enjoy being victims so much."

But even in this unbecoming, self-pitying side of Barca, there's a becoming side. Contrast Barca to Celtic or Rangers. The Scottish fans consider one another enemy tribes with inferior beliefs, who don't really deserve to occupy their town. It is stunning that, for all the rage toward Real, Barca fans feel so little animus toward the supporters of the club. There are scant examples of Barca hooligans battling Real. That's because they don't hate an opposing group of people; they feel rage toward an idea, the idea of Castilian centralism. And you can't beat up an idea.

Without a group of enemies to focus attention, there's an aimless, scattershot quality to the hatred of Barca fans. Consequently, they turn their rage on themselves as often as they turn it on others. During my visit, I watched the city rise up against the club's Dutch manager, Louis van Gaal. The city has a particularly robust press covering the club. Two daily sports papers have no other obvious purpose than expending approximately 280 pages each week delving into every bit of the club's minutiae. For months they devoted this space to vilifying Van Gaal. A typical story analyzes lunches consumed by the Dutch coach, alongside photographs documenting the growth of his belly. When he sits in the thirteenth row of the team plane, reporters interpret this as a sign of his poor judgment and imminent demise. Remarkably, this only begins to chart the Catalan media landscape and its hatreds. A weekly TV segment parodies Barca, using puppets to produce cruelly cutting send-ups of players and management, regularly portraying Van Gaal as a pile of bricks topped by a mop.

For a week, fans held anti–Van Gaal rallies in front of the Camp Nou. At times, the hecklers turned so vile, so personal, and so distracting that Van Gaal interrupted his training sessions and moved them to another, more private pitch. When I visited the protestors, they looked to be mostly a group of middle-aged men. They stood behind a black iron gate and shouted toward the field, about thirty yards away. Although they only numbered about two dozen, they amplified magnificently. They didn't have a single message, just insults and quixotic demands for new lineups and new strategies. Because they had been protesting for a week already—and their demand that Van Gaal be fired seemed so close to being met—neither the team nor the media paid them much attention. They solemnly went about their business.

I tried to talk to these malcontents. A short stocky man with a combover in a sweater and blazer allowed himself to be momentarily distracted from his shouting. As I approached, his abuses came out so fast that I couldn't really follow him. It was an unseasonably warm Mediterranean day and he constantly wiped his brow dry with a handkerchief.

"Why are you so angry?" I asked.

He grabbed my forearm with one hand. It was hard to know if this was a gesture of hostility or intimacy. In the moment, he might not have known himself.

"We hate him so much, because we love Barca so much. It hurts."

9

How Soccer Explains
Islam's Hope

I.

The biggest stadium in Tehran, in the world for that matter, is the 120,000-seat Azadi. Its name comes straight from the lexicon of Orwellian Newspeak. Even though it translates as "freedom," it represents something close to the opposite. Ever since the Islamic revolution of 1979, females have been forbidden to watch soccer in the Azadi. This prohibition isn't exclusive to the venue or even to Iran. It applies in broad swaths of the Muslim world, where it holds without much controversy. But the fundamental fact of Iran is that it is not Saudi Arabia. During the last decades of the shahs, it hadn't locked its women in black burqas. They had been high government officials, writers, lawyers, and fans of the beautiful game.

With so many people flowing through the Azadi's turnstiles, it's impossible to ensure conformity with the finer points of Islamic law. Fans will curse in the foulest, most clearly verboten language. They will throw punches that can't be justified by any reasonable inter- pretation of the Koran. Some of these men are clean- shaven and dressed in suspiciously baggy clothes. Under closer inspection, it would become clear that these men aren't even really men. Risking severe pun- ishment, Tehran's women have been unable to let go of the Azadi. They have suppressed their breasts, tucked away their long hair, dressed in man's garb, and snuck into the stadium.

This corps of aggrieved, soccer-starved women, it is reported, included the daughters of important clerics, the only women in Iran who actually had a voice in the governance of the country. Their unceasing complaints apparently struck enough of a fatherly chord to over- come juristic precedent. In 1987, the country's spiritual and political dictator, Ayatollah Ruhollah Khomeini, issued a new fatwa that revised the regime's absolute prohibition of female fandom. Speaking through his long white beard, he decreed that women could watch soccer on television, which would carry games for the first time in the Islamic era, but still disallowed trips to the testosterone-laden stadium. And for a while, the Khomeini compromise satisfied all.

But even the mullah's rare stroke of Solomonic rea- soning couldn't placate the deep desires of the Iranian women. Like all good fans, they understood that televi- sion is a poor substitute for the real, flesh-and-blood experience. In hindsight, it was inevitable that women would demand to be let back into the nation's stadi- ums. Still, such a bold demand requires great courage

and pretext. The heroics of the national team in
November 1997 gave the women of Iran both.

Iran's campaign to qualify for the World Cup turned
on a single playoff game against Australia, played in
Melbourne. For most of the match, the Iranians
knocked the ball around as if their government had
ordered them to throw the match intentionally, to ward
off victory celebrations in Tehran that might spin dan-
gerously out of control. But in the last fifteen minutes
of World Cup qualifying—frantic, desperate
moments—the Iranians tossed off their lethargy and
struck two stunning, salvaging goals. Iran would
advance to the World Cup for the first time since
Khomeini's 747 returned the exiled ayatollah to Tehran
eighteen years earlier.

Because the regime possesses a Roman nose for
self-preservation, it began immediately bracing for celebrations, knowing that euphoric people take leave of
their rationality, and without rationality guiding them,
they might be crazy enough to take to the barricades.
Already, the soccer scene had begun to reflect the aspirations for a new, more liberal Iran—the same spirit
that had catapulted the reformer Mohammad Khatami
to the presidency a few months earlier. For the first
time in the history of the Islamic republic, a foreign
coach led the squad, a Brazilian named Valdeir Vieira.
When he paced the sideline, he wore a necktie—a
fashion that the shahs had pushed as an emblem of
modern Iran and the clerics had rejected as a European
imposition. Many of Vieira's players made their careers
in European and Asian leagues, hopeful examples of
Iran interacting with the global economy.

Indeed, the government had been right to feel anxious. After the victory, the streets of Tehran filled with revelers. Their joy led them to dispense with the official morality. Dancing and drinking and western pop music, normally confined to homes, the private sphere, became the stuff of public celebration. If the revelers had been men, that might have been one thing. But in the well-heeled neighborhoods, and especially among the young, the celebrants reveled in mixed company. Some women threw off the *hijab* and partied without any of the mandated head coverings. When the *basiji,* members of the religious paramilitary militia, arrived to shut down the demonstrations, they were persuaded to join the roistering themselves.

Some delicate defusing was now in order. The government asked the team to meander back from Australia, taking a leisurely layover in Dubai, buying time for the situation in Tehran to cool down. Radio broadcasts warned citizens against secular celebrations that give Allah short shrift. Other messages specifically appealed to the women of the country, our "dear sisters," urging them to stay home during the homecoming celebrations.

When the team finally returned, three days later, the government held the celebration in the Azadi. The heroes arrived in the stadium via helicopters, as if Silvio Berlusconi had planned the event. But the real spectacle wasn't inside the stadium. Thousands of women defied the state's pleas and gathered on the other side of the Azadi's gates, in the 27-degree chill. As the anthropologist Christian Bromberger has reported, when the police refused to admit these women to the stadium, they began shouting "Aren't we part of this nation? We want to celebrate too. We aren't ants." Fearing the horde, the police let three thousand women into special seating, segregated from the rest of the stadium. But what about the two thousand women on the other side of the turnstile who hadn't wormed their way into the Azadi? The admission of their dear sisters did nothing to placate them. Determined to get their own piece of the celebration, they broke through the police gates and muscled their way into the stadium. Intent on avoiding a major fracas that could steer the raw emotions of the day in a dangerous direction, the police had no choice but to overlook their entry and concede defeat.

II.

When future historians write about the transformation of the Middle East, they will likely wax lyrical about this moment, which already has come to be known as the "football revolution." Like the Boston Tea Party, it will go down as the moment when the people first realized that they could challenge their tyrannical rulers. For the Iranians, the event has served as the model uprising, so much so that every subsequent high stakes World Cup qualifying match has led Iranians into the streets. Over time, the political subtext of these outpourings has become increasingly explicit. During the 2002 campaign, with each Iranian win—over Saudi Arabia, over Iraq, over the United Arab Emirates—festive fans chanted *"Zindibad azadi"* (long live freedom) and "We love America." But even this may underestimate the significance of the football revolution. It is more than an event. The football revolution holds the key to the future of the Middle East. This future could be discerned in the waving of the pre-Islamic national flag, the graffiti that praised the "noble people of Iran," and the celebrants' shouting of the name of Reza Pahlavi, the exiled son of the late shah—the roots of a nationalist uprising against Islam.

But is the football revolution the revolution that the U.S. wants? Not so long ago, secular nationalism looked like the great enemy in the Middle East. Dictators like Gamal Nasser, Muammar Qaddafi, and Hafez Assad were the biggest thorns in America's side, sponsoring hijacking and making war against Israel. In the eighties, however, these Arab nationalists fell upon tough times. They no longer could turn to the Soviet Union for patronage, and Gulf War I exposed how Americans could easily crush even the most powerful of this bunch. What's more, since the days of Nasser, these secularists had competed with Islamic movements funded by Saudi Arabia. Now, with the nationalists on the ropes, Hamas, Hezbollah, al-Qaeda, and radical Wahabi preachers have gained a serious upper hand in their battle for hegemony over the Muslim mind.

No doubt, the old dictators have caused many headaches, but America basically knew how to deal with them. It could play them off one another, and ultimately dismiss them as relatively harmless buffoons. Islamists, on the other hand, were an unfamiliar, uncontainable problem. How to turn the tide against

them? One answer has been to inject more globalization into the region. But so far it hasn't worked. In
places like Pakistan, a proliferation of KFC and Bolly-
wood movies has arguably aggravated the problem. By
displaying the western way of life, they draw attention
to the Islamic world's own humiliating lack of modernity. Another answer to the problem of Islamism, the
neo-conservative solution, proposes that the U.S.
aggressively push the Middle East toward democracy.
But the mere fact that the U.S. is the only force seriously committed to democratizing means that blind
hatred for the messenger will undermine the message.
The football revolution shows that the best antidote to
Islamism might not be something new, but something
old—a return to secular nationalism.

Indeed, the football revolution presages a promising
scenario: That people won't accede to theocracy forever,
especially when they can remember an era of greater lib-
erty before clerical rule. When they revolt, they might
fleetingly plead for American help, but they'll mostly
rise up in the name of their nation. We might not always
agree with the new nationalists—and they might take
their rhetorical shots at the U.S.—but they may be the
only viable alternative to government by Islam.

III.

The history of modern Iran can be told as the history of
Iranian soccer. It begins just after World War I with
Shah Reza the Great, King of Kings, Shadow of the
Almighty, God's Vicar and the Center of the Universe,

founder of the Pahlavi dynasty. Reza Khan, the man who would become Reza Shah at the ripe age of forty-seven, wasn't born to the palace. He had been a semiliterate soldier from the provinces who made his name leading a band of Russian-trained Cossacks. But in the eyes of the British, who lapped at the pool of Iranian oil and tried to quietly run the country, he was the perfect cipher—a man without political ambitions, accustomed to taking orders. In 1921, the general Sir Edmund Ironside, stationed in Tehran, humbly suggested that Reza might want to seize power. The old government had grown too nationalist and unreliable for Ironside's taste. With the British blessing, Reza's coup was a fait accompli. Four years later, Reza received the ultimate reward for his cooperation. He sent the old monarch packing to Europe, assumed his lengthy title and the full trappings of royalty. It was quite a leap for a simple village boy to make. But, as the British will attest, he proved to be far less of a pliant bumpkin than first imagined. He would use the military as his blunt instrument for remaking Persian society in the image of Prussian society, a modern nation to compete with Europe. Like his other role model, the great Turkish modernizer Kemal Atatürk, he built roads and railways and trampled traditional practices, belittling the mullahs and banning the chador. He legislated that men trash their robes and don proper western suits. To make a modern nation, he wanted to create a modern Iranian man who understood the values of hygiene, manly competition, and cooperation.

He became an enthusiastic proponent of physical education, a bow in the direction of German gymnastics, which he encoded in school curricula. Soccer soon became the regime's activity of choice. Reza Shah ordered the armed forces to play matches, even in the provinces, where European shoes hadn't yet made an appearance. "By the mid-1920s," as the incisive historian Houchang Chehabi has put it, "football had become a symbol of modernization, and soon the game was promoted at the highest levels of the state."

Just like Reza Shah himself, soccer owed its initial strength to the British. The Iranian elite had learned the game in missionary schools run by foreigners. And the Iranian masses learned the game by standing on the touchline and watching employees of the Anglo-Persian Oil Company. The idea of modernization in general, and soccer in particular, represented a shock to the Islamic system. Even though Reza Shah suppressed the clerics, they still waged a quiet resistance. In the villages, mullahs ordered the stone pelting of Iranian soccer players. By playing in British uniforms, the Iranians had slipped into shorts and out of compliance with shari'a, which dictates that men cover their legs from the navel to the knees.

But the old ways didn't stand a chance against the might of the modernizers, backed by the powerful state. Reza Shah's regime seized lands from mosques and converted them into football fields. Over time the state's enthusiasm for the game grew even greater. Where Reza Shah embraced the game for largely theoretical reasons, his son adored it with the passion of a purist. The crown prince Mohammad Reza Pahlavi played it at the Rosey School in Switzerland. Returning home in 1936, he lined up as a striker for the officers'

school he attended. When the British forced Reza Shah
to abdicate the peacock throne to his young son in 1941,
after he stupidly made himself cozy with the Nazis,
they enthroned the biggest football fanatic in the land.

Even though Iran was far from both the Asian and
European fronts, the Pahlavi push toward modernity
suffered a major setback with the economic disloca-
tions of World War II. In the country's weakened condition, foreign influences—still the British and
increasingly the American—became as pronounced as
ever, culminating in the CIA-led coup that ousted the
democratically elected prime minister Mohammad
Mossadegh in 1953. In the cities, both the socialist intelligentsia and traditional clerics began to assert themselves. Important matters of state weighed on the new
shah's mind. Nevertheless, as a devoted fan, he couldn't
tolerate losses that the Iranian national team suffered
in the 1950s. He began devoting resources to the creation of a great team.

In the second decade of his rule, the hard work paid
off. As part of the regime's continued program of
hyperkinetic growth and modernization, the newly
industrialized cities filled with millions of migrants
from the provinces. These arrivals, for the first time
enjoying a respite from the 24/7 grind of agriculture,
began to fill their leisure time with soccer. The newly
urbanized who couldn't wrangle tickets to the stadium
watched soccer on television—a medium that became
increasingly mass in the late sixties. But the popularity
of the sport rests largely on a single match played
against Israel in the wake of the 1967 war. Unlike the
rest of the Muslim world, the Iranians had a quiet

alliance with the Jewish state that withstood the tumult of the late sixties. (Israel has often had great success cultivating non-Arab allies on the fringes of the Muslim world.) Because of this alliance, Iranians didn't join with the other Muslim states, which had refused to even take the athletic field with Israelis.

The game was played as part of the quadrennial Asian Nations Cup. While the regime kept up relations with Israel, the Iranian people weren't entirely on the same page. Earlier in the tournament, when Israel played Hong Kong, Iranians pelted Jewish supporters with bottles. As Houchang Chehabi has reported, the game with Israel was a case study in ugliness. Fans released balloons covered in swastikas. They chanted, "Goal number two is in the net—a score. Moshe Dayan's poor ass is ripped and sore."

Many theories explain the logic behind the shah's decision to permit this contest to go forward. Many Iranians persuasively argue that the shah organized the match to harmlessly divert anti-Israeli sentiment. Others contend that the Israelis threw the match, 2–1, to buck up their friend, the shah. Whatever the shah's rationale, Iran's victory acquired a mythic significance. Pop singers enshrined it in song. Players became national icons, whose jukes and crosses were recreated by children in thousands of rag-ball street games.

If the regime had subtly used the game against Israel to bolster itself, its exploitation was more obvious in the years that followed. The game boomed in the seventies, with intense club rivalries forming. Members of the royal family glommed onto the newfangled popularity and began publicly rooting for the club Taj

(Crown). To cover the monarchy's bases, the shah's wife pulled for Taj's great rival, Persepolis. With the monarchy so closely identified with soccer, the regime's Islamist opponents inevitably targeted it, often disrupting games to stage their protests.

The shah's regime had many faults, especially handling its opponents with undeniable brutality. But its greatest shortcoming, the one that did it in, was the shah's modernization program. He pushed the country too hard, too fast, to become urban and industrial. Centuries of Persian life were uprooted and overhauled in the course of a generation of fevered transformation. When the revolutionaries ousted the shah in 1979, however, they tried hard to reverse the sporting symbol of this modernization program. They appropriated the soccer field at Tehran University, reversing the seizures made by Reza Shah, and used it as a staging ground for Friday prayers. They nationalized the soccer clubs, changing Taj into Esteghlal (Independence) and Persepolis into Piroozi (Victory). In their papers and pamphlets, the ascetic puritans made it clear that they considered soccer to be a debased calling. A typical revolutionary fulmination read: "Would it not have been better if instead of clowning around like the British and the Americans in order to 'shine' in international arenas, [the players] shone in the company of the brothers of the . . . jihad in our villages, where the simplest amenities are lacking? Have all our political, economic, and cultural problems been solved that we have turned to sport?"

IV.

In a very brief period, the Islamic regime managed to virtually eliminate Iranian pop culture, purging the divas and crooners, rejecting any movie that showed excessive flesh. But when this clampdown extended to soccer, the regime's position became untenable. It put the new government in direct opposition to a great passion of the Iranian people. And very quickly, the mullahs realized that eradicating soccer wasn't worth the political price. Since the clerics couldn't ruin soccer, they did the next best thing. They tried to co-opt it and milk the game for all its worth. For a time, agents of the regime infiltrated crowds of fans and attempted to lead chants praising Allah. The regime also experimented with plastering its slogans on the placards that surround the pitch. Instead of flogging Toshiba and Coke, the boards screamed, "Down with the USA" and "Israel must be destroyed."

But the government probably didn't ever seriously imagine that these political messages could break through—even subliminally—to transfixed fans. In fact, the crowds did something close to the opposite of shaking their fists and yelping Islamic chants. They laughed the religious cheerleaders out of the stadium. An unequivocal message to get the mosque out of the sport that the state ultimately heard. The regime stopped shoveling agitprop into soccer. It began to chart a more realistic course with a focus on cutting its losses and limiting the un-Islamic influences that might accompany the game. In this, it has been extraordinarily savvy. For some games, it insists on a slight delay in the broadcast, so that the censors have time to weed out the crowd's foul language or political messages that might be overheard on television. For other games, it electronically softens fan noise to a barely audible din. During the 1998 World Cup, the Iranian government lived in dread of its exiled opponents, especially a group of quasi-Marxists called the People's Mujahideen, who filled the stadiums in France, bringing along banners and carefully preparing chants. To avoid transmitting their embarrassingly subversive messages, Iranian television didn't shoot any footage of the actual crowd. Instead, it edited in stock images, and not terribly convincing ones. The televised crowds were bundled in heavy winter coats, hardly attire suited to France in June.

So what does the regime fear from soccer? In a poignantly comic scene in the filmmaker Abbas Kiarostami's *Life Goes On*, set in the wake of an enormous earthquake, men struggle to adjust an antenna to receive a match between Austria and Scotland. These aren't, it should be noted, giants of contemporary soccer. But that's beside the point. Iranians crave international soccer because the game links them to the advanced, capitalist, un-Islamic West. When they broadcast games from the World Cup, they can't avoid seeing the placards on the side of the pitch that advertise PlayStation, Doritos, and Nike, a way of life that Iranians are forbidden to join. Conservatives understand this connection. In their papers, photo editors blot out the advertising that graces the chests of Western jerseys.

But again, there's only so much damage control that the conservatives can do. They can blot out the ads but not the players themselves. Any photo of David Beckham, for example, with his protean hair always shifting from buzz to mohawk to ponytail, represents an idea of freedom. It's an idea that Iranian players have picked up on. Almost to a man, the national team plays without beards and with carefully coifed hair. They are heartthrobs, and many of them have gone on to careers in Germany, England, Singapore, and other outposts of the global economy. They couldn't be more different from the ideal of pious Iranian masculinity that the clerics in the holy city of Qum would like to project.

The 1997 presidential election featured the great white hope, the cleric and intellectual Mohammad Khatami. In his writings, he'd argued the compatibility of Islam and liberalism. His supporters daydreamed aloud that his election would usher in a new era of democracy, civil society, free speech, and greater rights for women. While the hopes of so many rested on Khatami, most Iranians didn't allow themselves too much optimism. Khatami was the overwhelming underdog in the race. His opponent Ali Akbar Nateq-Nouri, also a cleric, came with the blessings of the nation's top mullah, Ayatollah Khameni, and represented the forces of establishment conservatism. And in Iran, the clerics can, almost at will, bring down their strong arm, using militias to force their way.

Khatami articulated bits and pieces of a more liberal agenda. But Iranian political discourse is hardly a model marketplace of ideas. Certain thoughts can't be shouted. They need to be conveyed with subtext and symbols, like the athletes surrounding a candidate.

Among Iranian leisure games and activities, the most ancient and venerated is the *zurkhaneh,* the strong house. More precisely, the *zurkhaneh* isn't a sport but a gymnasium where sport takes place—indigenous games that involve the hoisting of heavy objects and other displays of brute strength that bear resemblance to wrestling and weightlifting. The rituals of the *zurkhaneh* are carefully prescribed. Moves begin with praise of the prophet's family. Because of these Islamic roots, Iranian conservatives have an unsurprising affinity for the *zurkhaneh.* Their newspapers devote heaps of coverage to the sport—and basically ignore soccer. In his campaign, Nateq-Nouri stumped with wrestling champions and let his devotion to the sport be widely known.

Unwittingly, Nateq-Nouri had turned himself into Khatami's perfect foil. Without having to utter too many words about democracy or the West, Khatami could prove himself to the reform-starved Iranians by aligning himself with the soccer stadium. Khatami surrounded himself with famous players, who endorsed him. There's no way to gauge the full effect of this strategy. But the logic is clear enough. The burgeoning youth population of Iran looked West and toward soccer for inspiration. In their eyes, the alliance with soccer indicated where Khatami's feelings truly rested. In the end, Khatami surprised the public and took the presidency.

But winning the presidency and satisfying the high hopes of your supporters are two different matters. Unfortunately, Khatami could never fulfill the dreams of young, secularly inclined Iranians, because he was never the creature they imagined. He was an intellectual without the courage or power to fully challenge the ruling clerics. More important, he was a traditional cleric himself.

For the past three years, from time to time, discontent with Khatami has emerged from its subterranean home. Many of these occasions of dissent have followed World Cup–related matches. As always, the regime has tried to preempt these eruptions with token gestures. After a vital qualifier for the 2002 World Cup, the government baked a cake with 12,000 eggs, which it delivered across Tehran in refrigerated trucks. But sweets weren't enough to restore the faith of youth. They have begun to seek out an alternative to both mullahs and reformist mullahs like Khatami. So far, the alternative hasn't taken a clear shape, but there are signs of direction. There's considerable nostalgia among youth for the days of the shah, even if they themselves never lived through them. Bootleg tapes of pop stars from the past have circulated widely; the necktie has been in resurgence. It's the same impulse behind the football revolutionaries shouting the name of the shah's son.

What should the West make of the football revolution? It's plausible that it represents the inevitable challenge that globalization poses to Islam. But that can't be the whole story. Soccer thrives in much of the Muslim world without counteracting radicalism. Hezbollah sponsors a soccer team in Lebanon and has in the past bought broadcasting rights to the Asian Nations' Cup for its radio network. The Wahabi-oriented Gulf States have imported aging Western stars for one last paycheck to play in their leagues.

They have built princely arenas with marble and gold leaf, like the awesome, Bedouin-inspired King Fadh International Stadium in Riyadh.

What makes the football revolution different is that it has tapped into nationalist fervor and turned it against the state. As great as the Iranian commitment to Islam is the Iranian commitment to Iran—the two haven't always been one and the same. There's a recent history of secular nationalism that serves as an alternative. It might not be the optimal alternative, but for now it will have to do.

10

How Soccer Explains the American Culture Wars

I.

My soccer career began in 1982, at the age of eight. This was an entirely different moment in the history of American soccer, well before the youth game acquired its current, highly evolved infrastructure. Our teams didn't have names. We had jersey colors that we used to refer to ourselves: "Go Maroon!" Our coach, a bearded German named Gunther, would bark at us in continental nomenclature that didn't quite translate into English. Urging me to stop a ball with my upper body, he would cry out, "Use your breasts, Frankie!"

That I should end up a soccer player defied the time-tested laws of sporting heredity. For generations, fathers bequeathed their sporting loves unto their sons. My father, like most men of his baby boom age, had grown up madly devoted to baseball. Why didn't my dad adhere to the practice of handing his game to his son? The answer has to do with the times and the class to which my parents belonged, by which I mean, they were children of the sixties and we lived in the yuppie confines of Upper Northwest Washington, D.C., a dense aggregation of Ivy League lawyers with aggressively liberal politics and exceptionally protective parenting styles. Nearly everyone in our family's social set signed up their children to play soccer. It was the fashionable thing to do. On Monday mornings, at school, we'd each walk around in the same cheaply made pair of white shorts with the logo of our league, Montgomery Soccer Inc.

Steering your child into soccer may have been fashionable, but it wasn't a decision to be made lightly. When my father played sandlot baseball, he could walk three blocks to his neighborhood diamond. With soccer, this simply wasn't possible. At this early moment in the youth soccer boom, the city of Washington didn't have any of its own leagues. My parents would load up our silver Honda Accord and drive me to fields deep in suburban Maryland, 40-minute drives made weekly across a landscape of oversized hardware stores and newly minted real estate developments. In part, these drives would take so long because my parents would circle, hopelessly lost, through neighborhoods they had never before visited and would likely never see again.

As I later discovered, my parents made this sacrifice of their leisure time because they believed that soccer could be transformational. I suffered from a painful, rather extreme case of shyness. I'm told that it extended beyond mere clinging to my mother's leg. On the sidelines at halftime, I would sit quietly on the edge of the other kids' conversations, never really interjecting myself. My parents had hoped that the game might necessitate my becoming more aggressive, a breaking through of inhibitions.

The idea that soccer could alleviate shyness was not an idiosyncratic parenting theory. It tapped into the conventional wisdom among yuppie parents. Soccer's appeal lay in its opposition to the other popular sports. For children of the sixties, there was something abhorrent about enrolling kids in American football, a game where violence wasn't just incidental but inherent. They didn't want to teach the acceptability of violence, let alone subject their precious children to the risk of physical maiming. Baseball, where each batter must stand center stage four or five times a game, entailed too many stressful, potentially ego-deflating encounters. Basketball, before Larry Bird's prime, still had the taint of the ghetto.

But soccer represented something very different. It was a tabula rasa, a sport onto which a generation of parents could project their values. Quickly, soccer came to represent the fundamental tenets of yuppie parenting, the spirit of *Sesame Street* and Dr. Benjamin Spock. Unlike the other sports, it would foster self-esteem, minimize the pain of competition while still teaching life lessons. Dick Wilson, the executive director of the American Youth Soccer Organization since the early seventies, described the attitude this way: "We would like to provide the child a chance to participate in a less competitive, win-oriented atmosphere. . . . We require that teams be balanced; and that teams not remain intact from year to year, that they be dissolved and totally reconstituted in the next season. This is done to preclude the adults from building their own dynasty 'win at all cost' situations."

This was typical of the thinking of a generation of post-'60s parenting theories, which were an extension of the counterculture spirit—Theodor Adorno's idea that strict, emotionally stultifying homes created authoritarian, bigoted kids. But for all the talk of freedom, the sixties parenting style had a far less laissez-faire side, too. Like the 1960s consumer movement which brought American car seatbelts and airbags, the soccer movement felt like it could create a set of rules and regulations that would protect both the child's body and mind from damage. Leagues like the one I played in handed out "participation" trophies to every player, no matter how few games his (or her) team won. Other leagues had stopped posting the scores of games or keeping score altogether. Where most of the world accepts the practice of heading the ball as an essential element of the game, American soccer parents have fretted over the potential for injury to the brain. An entire industry sprouted to manufacture protective headgear, not that different-looking from a boxer's sparring helmet, to soften the blows. Even though very little medical evidence supports this fear, some youth leagues have prohibited headers altogether.

This reveals a more fundamental difference between American youth soccer and the game as practiced in the rest of the world. In every other part of the world, soccer's sociology varies little: it is the province of the working class. Sure, there might be aristocrats, like Gianni Agnelli, who take an interest, and instances like Barca, where the game transcendently grips the community. But these cases are rare. The United States is even rarer. It inverts the class structure of the game. Here, aside from Latino immigrants, the professional classes follow the game most avidly and the working class couldn't give a toss about it. Surveys, done by the sporting goods manufacturers, consistently show that children of middle class and affluent families play the game disproportionately. Half the nation's soccer participants come from households earning over $50,000. That is, they come from the solid middle class and above.

Elites have never been especially well liked in postwar American politics—or at least they have been easy to take swipes at. But the generation of elites that adopted soccer has been an especially ripe target. That's because they came through college in the sixties and seventies, at a time when the counterculture self-consciously turned against the stultifying conformity of what it perceived as traditional America. Even as this group shed its youthful radical politics, it kept some of its old ideals, including its resolute cosmopolitanism and suspicions of middle America, "flyover country." When they adopted soccer, it gave the impression that they had turned their backs on the American pastime. This, naturally, produced even more disdain for them—and for their sport.

Pundits have employed many devices to sum up America's cultural divisions. During the 1980s, they talked about the "culture war"—the battle over textbooks, abortion, prayer in school, affirmative action, and funding of the arts. This war pitted conservative defenders of tradition and morality against liberal defenders of modernity and pluralism. More recently this debate has been described as the split between "red and blue America"—the two colors used to distinguish partisan preference in maps charting presidential election voting. But another explanatory device has yet to penetrate political science departments and the national desks of newspapers. There exists an important cleavage between the parts of the country that have adopted soccer as its pastime and the places that haven't. And this distinction lays bare an underrated source of American cultural cleavage: globalization.

II.

Other countries have greeted soccer with relative indifference. The Indian subcontinent and Australia come to mind. But the United States is perhaps the only place where a loud portion of the population actively disdains the game, even campaigns against it. This anti-soccer lobby believes, in the words of *USA Today*'s Tom Weir, "that hating soccer is more American than apple pie, driving a pickup, or spending Saturday afternoons channel surfing with the remote control." Weir exaggerates the pervasiveness of this sentiment. But the cadre of soccer haters has considerable sway. Their influence rests primarily with a legion of prestigious sportswriters and commentators, who use their column inches to fulminate against the game, especially on the occasions of World Cups.

Not just pundits buried in the C Section of the paper, but people with actual power believe that soccer represents a genuine threat to the American way of life. The former Buffalo Bills quarterback Jack Kemp, one of the most influential conservatives of the 1980s, a man once mentioned in the same breath as the presidency, holds this view. In 1986, he took to the floor of the United States Congress to orate against a resolution in support of an American bid to host the World Cup. Kemp intoned, "I think it is important for all those young out there, who someday hope to play real football, where you throw it and kick it and run with it and put it in your hands, a distinction should be made that football is democratic, capitalism, whereas soccer is a European socialist [sport]."

Lovers of the game usually can't resist dismissing these critics as xenophobes and reactionaries intoxicated with a sense of cultural superiority, the sporting wing of Pat Buchanan's America First conservatism. For a time, I believed this myself. But over the years I've met too many conservatives who violently disagree with Kemp's grafting of politics onto the game. And I've heard too many liberals take their shots at soccer, people who write for such publications as the *Village Voice* and couldn't be plausibly grouped in the troglodyte camp of American politics. So if hatred of soccer has nothing to do with politics, conventionally defined, why do so many Americans feel threatened by the beautiful game?

For years, I have been collecting a file on this anti-soccer lobby. The person whose material mounts highest in my collection is the wildly popular radio shock jock Jim Rome. Rome arrived on the national scene in the mid-nineties and built an audience based on his self-congratulatory flouting of social norms. Rome has created his own subculture that has enraptured a broad swath of American males. They are united by their own vernacular, a Walter Winchell–like form of slang that Rome calls "smack," derived in part from the African American street and in part from the fraternity house. An important part of this subculture entails making fun of the people who aren't members of it. Rome can be cruelly cutting to callers who don't pass his muster, who talk the wrong kind of smack or freeze up on air. These putdowns form a large chunk of his programs. The topics of his rants include such far-ranging subject matter as the quackery of chiropractors, cheap seafood restaurants, and, above all, soccer.

Where specific events trigger most soccer hating— a World Cup, news of hooligan catastrophes that arrive over the wires—Rome doesn't need a proximate cause to break into a tirade. He lets randomly rip with invective. "My son is not playing soccer. I will hand him ice skates and a shimmering sequined blouse before I hand him a soccer ball. Soccer is not a sport, does not need to be on my TV, and my son will not be playing it." In moments of honesty, he more or less admits his illogic. "If it's incredibly stupid and soccer is in any way related, then soccer must be the root cause [of the stupidity]," he said in one segment, where he attacked the sporting goods manufacturer Umbro for putting out a line of clothing called Zyklon, the same name as the Auschwitz gas. (Zyklon translates as cyclone. By his logic, the words "concentration" or "camp" should be purged from conversational English for their Holocaust associations.) He often inadvertently endorses some repulsive arguments. One segment ripped into African soccer teams for deploying witch doctors. "So you can add this to the laundry list of reasons why I hate soccer," he frothed.

Such obvious flaws make it seem he is proud of his crassness, and that would be entirely in keeping with character. These arguments would be more easily dismissed were they the product of a single demented individual. But far smarter minds have devolved down to Rome's level. Allen Barra, a sportswriter for the *Wall Street Journal,* is one of these smarter minds. Usually, Barra distinguishes himself from his colleagues by making especially rarified, sharp arguments that follow clearly from the facts and have evidence backing his provocative claims. But on soccer, he slips from his moorings. He writes, "Yes, OK, soccer is the most 'popular' game in the world. And rice is the most 'popular' food in the world. So what? Maybe other countries can't afford football, basketball and baseball leagues: maybe if they could afford these other sports, they'd enjoy them even more."

Unlike Rome, Barra has some sense of why he flies off the handle on this subject. It has to do with his resentment of the game's yuppie promoters. He argues, "Americans are such suckers when it comes to something with a European label that many who have resisted thus far would give in to trendiness and push their kids into youth soccer programs." And more than that, he worries that the soccer enthusiasts want the U.S. to "get with the rest of the world's program."

As Barra makes clear, the anti-soccer lobby really articulates the same fears as Eurico Miranda and Alan

Garrison, a phobia of globalization. To understand their fears, it is important to note that both Barra and Rome are proud aficionados of baseball. The United States, with its unashamedly dynamic culture, doesn't have too many deeply rooted, transgenerational traditions that it can claim as its own. Baseball is one of the few. That's one reason why the game gets so much nostalgia-drenched celebration in Kevin Costner movies and Stephen Jay Gould books.

But Major League Baseball, let's face it, has been a loser in globalization. Unlike the NBA or NFL, it hasn't made the least attempt to market itself to a global audience. And the global audience has shown no hunger for the game. Because baseball has failed to master the global economy, it has been beat back by it. According to the Sporting Goods Manufacturers Association of America, the number of teens playing baseball fell 47 percent between 1987 and 2000. During that same period, youth soccer grew exponentially. By 2002, 1.3 million more kids played soccer than Little League. And the demographic profile of baseball has grown ever more lily white. It has failed to draw African Americans and attracts few Latinos who didn't grow up playing the game in the Caribbean. The change can also be registered in the ballot box that matters most. Nielsen ratings show that, in most years, a World Series can no longer draw the same number of viewers as an inconsequential Monday night game in the NFL.

It's not surprising that Americans should split like this over soccer. Globalization increasingly provides the subtext for the American cultural split. This isn't to say America violently or even knowingly divides over globalization. But after September 11 opened new debates over foreign policy, two camps in American politics have clearly emerged. One camp believes in the essential tenets of the globalization religion as preached by European politicians, that national governments should defer to institutions like the UN and WTO. These tend to be people who opposed the war in Iraq. And this opinion reflects a worldview. These Americans share cultural values with Europeans—an aggressive secularism, a more relaxed set of cultural mores that tolerates gays and pot smoking—which isn't surprising, considering that these Americans have jobs and tourist interests that put them in regular contact with the other side of the Atlantic. They consider themselves to be part of a cosmopolitan culture that transcends national boundaries.

On the other side, there is a group that believes in "American exceptionalism," an idea that America's history and singular form of government has given the nation a unique role to play in the world; that the U.S. should be above submitting to international laws and bodies. They view Europeans as degraded by their lax attitudes, and worry about the threat to American culture posed by secular tolerance. With so much relativism seeping into the American way of life, they fret that the country has lost the self-confidence to make basic moral judgments, to condemn evil. Soccer isn't exactly pernicious, but it's a symbol of the U.S. junking its tradition to "get with the rest of the world's program."

There are many conservatives who hate relativism, consider the French wussy, and still adore soccer. But it's not a coincidence that the game has become a small touchstone in this culture war.

III.

I wish that my side, the yuppie soccer fans, were blameless victims in these culture wars. But I've been around enough of America's soccer cognoscenti to know that they invite abuse. They are inveterate snobs, so snobbish, in fact, that they think nothing of turning against their comrades. According to their sneering critique, their fellow fans are dilettantes without any real understanding of the game; they are yuppies who admire soccer like a fine slab of imported goat cheese; they come from neighborhoods with spectacularly high Starbucks-per-capita, so they lack any semblance of burning working-class passion.

This self-loathing critique can be easily debunked. I've seen the counterevidence with my own eyes. In the spring of 2001, the U.S. national team played Honduras in Washington's Robert Francis Kennedy stadium. This vital World Cup qualifying match had generated the packed, exuberant stadium that the occasion deserved. Fans wore their nation's jersey. Their singing and stomping caused the steel and concrete to undulate like the Mexican wave. In a country with lesser engineering standards, it would have been time to worry about a stadium collapse. On the field, stewards scampered to pick up scattered sneakers. Fans had removed them and thrown them at the opposing goalkeeper, a small gesture of homage to the madness of

Glasgow and the passion of Barcelona. They mercilessly booed the linesman, softening him up by insulting his slut of a mother. It might not have quite ascended to the atmospheric wonders of a game played by the English national team, but it wasn't far from that mark.

There is, however, an important difference between a home game in London and Washington. The majority of English fans will root for England. In Washington, more or less half the stadium wore the blue-and-white Honduran jersey, and they were the ones who shouted themselves hoarse and heaved their shoes. The American aspiration of appearing in the World Cup rested on this game. But on that day, the Washington stadium might as well have been in Tegucigalpa.

Traveling through Europe, you hear the same complaint repeated over and over: Americans are so "hypernationalistic." But is there any country in the world that would tolerate such animosity to their national team in their own national capital? In England or France or Italy, this would have been cause for unleashing hooligan hell.

Nor were the American fans what you'd expect of a hegemonic power. The *Washington Post* had published a message from the national soccer federation urging us to wear red shirts as a sign of support—and to clearly distinguish ourselves from the Hondurans. But most American soccer fans don't possess a red USA jersey and aren't about to go down to the sporting goods store to buy one. They do, however, own red Arsenal, Man U., and Ajax jerseys, or, in my case, an old Barcelona one, that they collected on continental travels. While we were giving a patriotic boost, we couldn't help revealing our Europhilic cosmopolitanism.

I mention this scene because many critics of globalization make America the wicked villain in the tale. They portray the U.S. forcing Nike, McDonald's and *Baywatch* down the throats of the unwilling world, shredding ancient cultures for the sake of empire and cash. But that version of events skirts the obvious truth: Multinational corporations are just that, multinational; they don't represent American interests or American culture. Just as much as they have changed the tastes and economies of other countries, they have tried to change the tastes and economy of the United States. Witness the Nike and Budweiser campaigns to sell soccer here. No other country has been as subjected to the free flows of capital and labor, so constantly remade by migration, and found its national identity so constantly challenged. In short, America may be an exception, but it is not exceptionally immune to globalization. And we fight about it, whether we know it or not, just like everyone else.

Note on Sources

There's not much written on the connection between Serbian hooligans and the Balkan wars. As far as I know, the anthropologist Ivan Colovic is the only one to cover this ground. His work can be found in a translated collection, *Politics of Identity in Serbia: Essays in Political Anthropology* (New York: New York University Press, 2002). Colovic mines obscure sources—pulp fiction, television shows, sports pages—and comes back with profound observations. Unlike many cultural critics, however, he has as good a grasp of reality as obtuse theory.

My chapter on Glasgow owes a huge debt to Bill Murray, an Australian academic, who has produced the two most rigorous histories of the Celtic-Rangers rivalry: *The Old Firm: Sectarianism, Sport and Society in Scotland* (Edinburgh: John Donald, 1984) and *The Old Firm in the New Age: Celtic and Rangers Since the Souness Revolution* (Edinburgh: Mainstream Publishing, 1998). Some of my anecdotes in this chapter come from Stuart Cosgrove's *Hampden Babylon* (Edinburgh: Canongate Books, 1991). T. M. Devine has edited a collection of essays on the sectarian divide called *Scotland's Shame?* (Edinburgh: Mainstream, 2000).

There's sadly little written on the Jewish soccer renaissance. There's John Bunzl's *Hoppauf Hakoah: Jüdischer*

Sport in Österreich von den Anfängen bis in die Gegenwart
(Vienna: Janus, 1987) and the Vienna's Jewish
Museum's exhibition catalog *Hakoah: Ein Jüdischer
Sportverein in Wien, 1909–1995* (Vienna: Der Apfel,
1995). In addition, there is an important book com-
memorating the club's fiftieth anniversary: Otto Bahr's
50 Jahre Hakoah (Tel Aviv: Verlagskomitee Hakoah Tel
Aviv, 1959). Hungarian soccer has received a little bit
more attention. The historian, cultural critic, and MTK
fan Tamás Krausz has a superb essay on his favorite
club's ethnic heritage that can be found online at
http://eszmelet.tripod.com/angol1/krauszang1.html.
Miklós Hadas and Viktor Karády have also published a
history of MTK's Jewishness that can found at
http://www.replika.c3.hu/1718/hadas.htm. David Winner's *Brilliant Orange: The Neurotic Genius of Dutch
Football* (London: Bloosmbury, 2000) is one of the great
books written about the sport. I particularly recom-
mend his chapter on Ajax and the Jews. The same subject gets a more comprehensive treatment in Simon
Kuper's *Ajax, The Dutch, The War: Football in Europe
During the Second World War* (London: Orion, 2003).
Finally, there's lots written about Max Nordau, but I
leaned heavily on Michael Stanislawski's *Zionism and
the Fin de Siècle: Cosmopolitanism and Nationalism for
Nordau to Jabotinsky* (Berkeley: University of California
Press, 2001).

Chapters from Alan Garrison's manuscript can be
found at *http://www.chelsea-desktop-wallpaper.co.uk/.* For
an understanding of the recent transformation of the
English game, I relied on David Conn's *The Football
Business* (Edinburgh: Mainstream, 1997).

Alex Bellos's *Futebol, the Brazilian Way* (London: Bloomsbury, 2002) provided an account of corruption in the Brazilian game. I frequently found myself referring to *Péle: His Life and Times* (London: Robson Books, 2000). Much of my knowledge of Brazilian history derives from Joseph A. Page's *The Brazilians* (Reading, Massachusetts: Perseus Books, 1995) and Marshall Eakin's *Brazil: The Once and Future Country* (New York: St. Martin's Press, 1997).

Tobias Jones's *The Dark Heart of Italy: Travels through Time and Space Across Italy* (London: Faber and Faber, 2003) has a superb chapter on the Italian game. I've found no better survey of Italian politics than Patrick McCarthy's *The Crisis of the Italian State: From the Origins of the Cold War to the Fall of Berlusconi* (New York: St. Martin's Press, 1995).

Jimmy Burns's *Barca: A People's Passion* (London, Bloomsbury, 1998) does a marvelous job synthesizing the history of my beloved club. Phil Ball's *Morbo: The Story of Spanish Football* (London: WSC Books, 2001) was also a useful source.

For Iranian soccer, I depended on the scholarship of Houchang Chehabi. He allowed me to view an advanced copy of his essay "The Politics of Football in Iran." I also relied on his essay "The Juggernaut of Globalization: Sport and Modernization in Iran," published in volume 19 of *The International Journal of the History of Sport*. Christian Bromberger's essay "Troisième mi-temps pour le Football Iranien" can be found online (*http://www.mondediplomatique.fr/1998/04 /BROMBERGER/10280*).

Finally, I want to express my gratitude to Peterjon Cresswell and Simon Evans for putting together *The*

Rough Guide's European Football: A Fan's Handbook
(London: Penguin Books, 1999). I followed their
anthropological insights and travel tips across the continent. Depressingly, many pages from my edition slowly
came unglued from their binding and ultimately
floated away in a Vienna breeze. Simon Kuper's *Football
Against the Enemy* (London: Orion, 1994) was an inspiration for this book.

Acknowledgments

When I first tentatively mentioned the idea of this book to my agent, Rafe Sagalyn, I expected him to laugh it off. Instead, he told me to drop everything and write a proposal. And after I dropped everything, he never dropped me. I am so grateful for his loyalty, advice, and friendship. Tim Duggan, my editor, isn't even a soccer fan—which makes me even more appreciative of his commitment to this book. Book editing, as a discipline, takes a lot of knocks. Editors are said to have become bean counters and tools of marketing departments. But Tim is wonderfully old school. He can structure a chapter, tease out an argument, and walk a writer back from the literary ledge. He cares about ideas.

Gabriele Marcotti is my learned soccer guru. He doesn't just know his football, he knows his politics, economics, and culture. I'm so grateful for the many hours he spent with me on the phone. Thanks to him, I also found a network of journalists who opened their Rolodexes and shared their considerable reportorial expertise: Ben Lyttleton, Ian McGarry, and Graham Hunter. In Italy, Gabriele connected me with Aurelio Capaldi, who generously led me by the hand through Rome.

My cousin Marcelo Waimberg took two weeks off

his job to serve as my translator. Those were the two best weeks I spent working on this book. Even though he is an engineer, he has the mind and soul of a journalist—skeptical and inquisitive. My entire Brazilian clan continually sets new, unsurpassable benchmarks for hospitality. I spent several weeks living in Jacques and Nair Waimberg's guest bedroom.

On my travels, I found myself in the protective grasp of an international fraternity of journalists. A thousand thank-yous to Fiachra Gibbons, Angelique Chrisafis, Pat Kane, Andrew Jennings, Richard Wilson, Gustavo Poli, Juca Kfouri, João Carlos Assumpcão, Mario Magalhães, Raul Lores, Leonardo Pinto da Silva, Dejan Nikolic, Dejan Anastasijevic, Ivan Colovic, Kevin Mousley, John Carlin, Taras Hordiyenko, Mike Ticher, Grant Wahl, Gunnar Persson, Joan Poqui, Beppe Severgnini, and Tommaso Pellizzari. I'm also grateful for the help of Andy Markovits, Aleksandar Hemon, Colin Jose, Houchang Chehabi, Amir Afkhami, Afshin Molavi, John Bunzl, Viktor Karády, Péter Szegedi, Sándor Laczkó, Tim Parks, Mario Sconcerti, Martin Vogel, Alex Alexiev, Eric Gordy, Walter Laqueur, Doug McGray, David Brett Wasser, and John Efron. (Efron came through with essential information about Tottenham's Jewishness.) It pains me to know that I'm not expressing proper gratitude to dozens of others who provided boosts along the way.

In addition to Tim Duggan, this book benefited immeasurably from the eyes and pens of several dear friends: Bryan Curtis, Jodi Kantor, David Plotz, Jay Tolson, and Jason Zengerle. I'm embarrassed to think of how much they improved my copy. My editors at the

New Republic—Peter Beinart, Chris Orr, and Martin Peretz—gave me eight months leave to kick-start this project.

My family suggested the idea for this book on a vacation to Barcelona, as we sat in the upper tier of the Camp Nou. For the next two years, my parents and brothers talked me through outlines and read drafts. Finally, more than HarperCollins, my wife was this book's patron. Without her encouragement and support—not to mention understanding—I would have never traveled around the world for this book. I loved the hours we spent holed up in the home office as she read through the manuscript—and I love her.

Index